A Walk in the Perfumed Garden
James Ayton

Published by Boleyn Publications at Draft2Digital
Copyright 2023 James Ayton
Boleyn, Norwich, England, NR5 0UF

This book is sold subject to the condition that it shall not, by way of trade or otherwise, be lent, resold, hired out or otherwise circulated without the publisher's prior consent in any form of binding or cover other than that in which it is published and without a similar condition including this condition being imposed on the subsequent purchaser.

JAMES AYTON

First published in 2023

Author's Acknowledgments

The author acknowledges quotations from texts of the following:
Lady Chatterley's Lover by D H Lawrence.
Penguin Essentials edition Pub 2011
www.greenpenguin.co.uk
Copyright: the estate of Frieda Lawrence Ravagli 1993
The Perfumed Garden
Translation by Sir Richard Burton
Published in 1963 by Panther Books
Married Love by Marie Carmichael Stopes
Copyright, 1918. The Critic & Guide Co.
Collected Poems of Philip Larkin
Edition published in 2003
Faber & Faber Ltd
The Bible According to Spike Milligan
Copyright 1993. Michael Joseph
Published by the Penguin Group

Dedicated to the passionate.

They shall find Heaven with every orgasm.

Contents

In the beginning

I was fated to find solace in a garden. My ancestors were gardeners to the aristocracy but my garden was unlike anything tended by those forebears. It was an escape from reality; a place where I embraced hardy blossoms; a sensual garden where I wondered at maturing succulents but desisted from plucking anything until it was ripe.

At the close of my teenage years I met the girl of my dreams and discovered "The Perfumed Garden", a bold new book of inspiration. The critics called it "a eulogy of love, a song of sensual delights, a collection of joyous imaginings and a work of rare and curious erotic knowledge". I savoured both these experiences in 1963, the year I was set up for life.

This explicit essay of romance was prompted by my grandchildren. They asked what traditional romance was like in 'the dinosaur age' of my youth, before gender recognition became a confusing issue: "Grandad, how did you meet Grandma Alison and did you have something for the weekend"

Alison Keeler and I met in a darkened auditorium and we enjoyed something every weekend! But envious friends warned I would be 'consumed' by my voluptuous new girlfriend and blown out in bubbles! Alison and I may have been poles apart in some partisan arenas but we were devoted in love.

When we bonded our teenage lives in 1963 the Keeler namesake was making international headlines through the political escapades of Christine, an attractive show girl. At the same time, romantic liaisons for lovers were known as 'dirty weekends' while 'something' was a euphemism for contraceptives. Before society became "permissive" and let its hair down, condoms and women's necessities were rarely mentioned, skimpily advertised and not openly available.

Our generation swelled the vanguard of the 'Swinging Sixties', those delightful few years when life was laid bare by the power of love. A nation, which had prospered on being disgusted and embarrassed by all things sexual, gradually shed most stigmas of its puritanical upbringing and delivered 'the permissive society'; the era when hems of skirts were raised and symbolical knickers were discarded!

Chapter 1

Early in manhood a wise man advised me to meet the mother of any serious girlfriend. Heeding the advice would show what I might wake up to each morning in thirty years' time! Before I had chance to plan the encounter I was invited, or rather summoned, to meet Alison's parents.

My prospective mother-in-law, Hannah Keeler, a farmer's wife, was a formidable woman of stout build; stern, yet amenable; disciplined, argumentative and God-faring. She had firm views on all things procreative and was well aware of men's desires, comparing most of us to stallions, "needing a bit and bridle". But she in turn was a farmer's daughter with a crupper as broad as a mare's!

Alison's father, while of lesser stature, maintained control of his wife for most of the time! Hannah adamantly denied 'wearing the trousers' in their marriage; certainly not the kind being pulled on each day! Hannah was far from dainty but she was a man's woman.

Alison had inherited many of her mother's qualities and gone further by blossoming into an 'English rose' or in 'Pygmalion' terms, would have courted attention in social circles, higher than I was offering. Her impeccable life skills and graces in deportment had been acquired through a private education, paid for by her father. He worshipped Alison, according to Hannah, as any doting father would for his only child, wanting her to have the best of everything that life could offer. Hannah accused him of lavishing too much on their daughter but she was now resigned to assuming I would continue in the vogue!

I tried to summarise the future as my wise friend had guided. Alison had won my heart with her mature attributes and seemed to have inherited her mother's physique, resilience and mannerisms which set my mind in motion. Mother and daughter displayed similarities, each inheriting influences through sharing the Zodiac sign of Libra, with birthdays five days apart.

Hannah descended from a farming dynasty. She held a lifelong respect for equines and I accepted as complimentary her equation of my gender with stallions because she admired them as long as they responded to commands. As a little girl, at the start of World War 1, she had witnessed her father in tears when his prized shire horses were commandeered for service on the Flanders battlefront.

My inquisitiveness revealed Hannah as a woman whose life could have taken a different path. As a child, she learned to play the piano and harboured the ambition to be a school teacher but instead was fated to the servitude of farm work. As a strong and willing farmer's daughter it was her only means to guarantee an inheritance, so there was little chance of escape.

During the second war, with a shortage of men to cultivate the fields, Hannah became hardened to heavy farm work. Her working life was spent labouring in all weathers, seven days a week; milking cows, dealing with animal births or bringing in the sheaves at harvest. She was skilled at churning milk into butter and boasted the ability to cope with anything life threw at her while there was breath in her body. Towards the end of the war, she married and bore one child, rather late in her years; the girl who entered my 'garden of dreams' and would now complete the other half of my life.

Hannah's shapeliness came from a physique toughened by the graft of heavy farm labouring. She seemed wrongly attired for such tasks; in skirts or dresses and in all weathers. Her leisure clothes were always fashionable; hemlines almost above the knee, obviously led by the trends of Alison. She displayed ample hips, accentuating the broad beam of her 'crupper'. I had been led to understand she was formidably strong-willed and forthright but I soon assessed her bark was worse than her bite and the real bite was harnessed between her thighs. Hannah, really was a man's woman!

I questioned myself as to why I was paying my prospective mother-in-law such intimate attention. She was far beyond the age of what is termed as 'the older woman' when pondering flirtatious age differences. But I was merely visualising her as Alison in later life; as my wise friend had advised; "Get to see your girlfriend's mother before you go too far!"

Hannah would make ungracious flops into a deep sofa, causing her skirt to be drawn higher than intended; revealing thick support stockings, tethered by suspenders, anchored to corsets allowing generous lilywhite thighs to draw my straying eyes. I briefly glimpsed the gusset of white underwear packing a bulging 'mound of Venus' into a cushion-like protuberance, just before my view was hindered by the rapid crossing of her legs.

She would tug downwards on the skirt's hem every time she caught my gaze. Her attempts to thwart my view were futile and made me more inquisitive. She was not young enough to wear short skirts. I was nineteen; she was fifty five; comfortably married and I was about to become engaged to her daughter!

My observations were pre-empted having read "The Perfumed Garden". The translation of this ancient Arabian 'eulogy of love' made clear the duty of a devoted wife:

"She does not surrender herself to anybody but her husband, even if abstinence would kill her. She hides her secret parts and does not allow them to be seen; she is always elegantly attired, of the utmost personal propriety, and takes care not to let her husband see what might be repugnant to him".

During subsequent visits to the home I was made aware that Hannah harboured a simmering undercurrent. Alison knew our liaison had caused her mother 'a crisis' as she had taken a firm liking to me; so I was given to understand. Hannah was experiencing an excited jealousy and subconscious orgastic emotions. It was common knowledge that some mothers could become wishfully receptive on meeting a prospective son-in-law!

Hannah often commented on my first visit to the home. She had caught sight of me seeking the help of a neighbour having lost my way to the farm. Many times she reminded me of how I ran up the lane with my crop of fair hair "flopping around". Sometime later I was secretly informed I had made her feel 'unnecessary'; an age old expression meaning the excitement of my presence had caused a secretion in her underwear! My vulgar friends would have said she had 'creamed her knickers'.

Hannah's adulation for me was hardly mutual and a little difficult to comprehend. But I could not deny being aware of the shapely broadness of her beam and an occasional sparkle in the eye. Every desire of teenage days began to haunt me and if I was to be branded a stallion then Hannah was a mare in waiting!

Sometimes I drifted into moments of idle fantasy, standing as Hannah's stallion; eyeing her as the mare. Her legs were long with ample thighs; long legs heightened by the relative shortness of her torso. In this musing we were naked. Hannah was presenting a ravine-like vulva, inviting my entry. I grasped her hips and thrust into her as far as my erection would reach. Once more I was running up a narrowing country lane, only this time hemmed in by ample thighs, instead of hedgerows. She consumed and sapped all my energy as I ejaculated and delivered my seed; living up to the reputation she had bestowed on most of my gender. But she was the temptress; almost three times my age; an adulteress and I the adulterer, even before I had tampered with the virginity of her daughter! Then back to reality, I was grateful for my wise friend's advice. I imagined exactly what I would be waking up to, in the mornings, in forty years' time!

Having been raised in the beliefs that man had to woo woman, treat her with kindness and be gentle, I felt well-versed for my journey into courtship. Literature's historical lover, Casanova, and the legendary movie idol Rudolph Valentino were my role models. Likewise, I had often been accused of living in a dream world but I always trusted the scenarios of my imagination, like the storylines of my favourite movies, found only in a garden of dreams.

Chapter 2

"Of all the movie houses in town I was destined to walk into hers". I parodied an unforgettable line uttered by Hollywood's iconic Humphrey Bogart in his 1942 film, "Casablanca". As Rick Blaine he runs a café in Morocco's largest city, during wartime, where desperate refugees seek visas home to America.

When Rick's former lover turns up unexpectedly, in the guise of Swedish actress Ingrid Bergman, he delivered the immortal line: "Of all the gin joints, in all the towns, in all the world, she walks into mine." In this story, an enigmatic young woman was found sitting alone in a place I held sacred and we became lovers for the rest of our days.

The culture of film narrative influenced me from an early age. I found movie magic overwhelming and it gradually dictated the way I dealt with life. If it was in the movies, I wanted to do the same.

Parental control had governed my infrequent escapes to the cinema, simply deepening my desire to see more films. Then a much loved local "Cinema Paradiso" with its "garden of dreams", closed in 1960, the year I left school, gained my freedom and started work in the city.

As a child, I hated our capital town. I saw it as "Metropolis", a landmark, frightening movie of 1928; noisy and overpowering but now it was my place of work, and I became addicted to its buzz. Old school friends felt abandoned by me as they rarely made it to the capital, envying how I was now in the thick of life, "surrounded by all those girls".

But I was meeting very few girls as my leisure time was spent at any one of the city's "picture theatres". A cinema was the place where I hoped to take one of "those girls", not find one and she would have to be special, like women in the movies; like Ingrid Bergman! I was too busy getting to grips with a career.

Fulfilling an ambition nurtured since school days I worked at the local television studios where the corridors were an endless buzz of debutantes. These were the types of girls I was meeting daily, so I should have been in clover! But they were unlikely to associate with a lowly messenger boy, cranking to and fro on the company bicycle!

For the curiously intrigued I was paid handsomely to 'ride' an innuendos 'company bicycle'. But in my case it was the type with a small front wheel designed with a capacious carrier to accommodate weighty video tapes and films. 'Bicycles' of a female flirtatious nature, allegedly, were available to the more mature and experienced eligible chaps!

My friends had always considered me a boring bibliophile, keeping myself genned on chosen subjects; local history, cinemas and sex! Seven years had passed since I shared my classmates' excitement as we dealt with girls in the playground and built up a healthy appetite for the opposite sex. But unlike my school friends, I had escaped rurality, developing a passion for city life. I was well clear of the parental doorstep for my journey of a lifetime.

Early in my city-based career, 1963 emerged as a milestone year. In September, the new film to see was "Tom Jones" starring two rising names of the day, Albert Finney and Susannah York.

The bawdy tale from Henry Fielding's novel, set in England during the 18th century, told of a foundling who is raised by the local squire and marries his daughter after a series of adventures. The moment the film was on release, legendary critic, John Simon gave it a slaughtering review and I was a glutton to follow the critics:

"It is as though the camera had become a method actor: there are times when you wish you could buy, as on certain juke boxes, five minutes of silence.......Obviously a film which elicits such lyrical ejaculations cannot be all good".

A film eliciting "lyrical ejaculations" had to be seen. Despite the critique, "Tom Jones" was benefitting from success at the Oscars but more significant for me, it was showing at the city's iconic movie theatre, Oscar Deutsch's 1938 Odeon.

The Odeon was the first incursion into our city by the industry's adoption of brand marketing. Studying cinema architecture had been my special subject since school days, two places ahead of local history and sex. On a dull September Saturday afternoon in 1963 I headed off to the city.

Saturday afternoon audiences tended to be rather sparse. It was evident on this day when I entered the Odeon's colossal art deco auditorium and took my usual seat at the rear of the front circle, close to the central aisle. Selfishly, I could enjoy an uninterrupted view of the wide proscenium all but for one youngish woman, sitting alone, a row or so down the aisle and comfortably clear of my line of vision.

As the lights dimmed I settled contentedly into the supporting programme. Immediately, the woman began flicking her cigarette lighter, frantically, obviously desperate to smoke. There was a distracting flash with every flick but each time the lighter failed to ignite.

I had no real issue as smoking was the vogue everywhere in those years before health concerns, especially in cinemas. As children, we loved to see the projector beam highlighted by ascending clouds of exhaled smoke. It was part of the cinema experience but on this day the endless flicking distracted me. I just wanted her to light up, send some smoke into the beam and take me with it so I could immerse myself into the film.

In the auditorium's ambient light the lady appeared mature. Her mannerisms in attempting to light a cigarette displayed refinement so I moved gently from my seat to courteously offer help with the lighter. She welcomed my proposal and suggested I take the seat, temporarily, beside her. If a woman could be considered as sitting graciously this was such a woman and she radiated perfection.

From my basic knowledge of smoking, the cigarette lighter was of traditional design. In the dim light of the auditorium I found and prised open the little flap to access the fuel chamber, revealing its pad of wool, normally soaked in fuel. It was dry and odourless and may not to have been filled for some time, if ever. Momentarily, it crossed my mind that I might have encountered a virgin smoker and broken a seal!

For the benefit of doubt I attempted to compress the padding in the hope of squeezing any remaining fuel towards the wick, using a ball point pen, the only implement to hand. Having no success, I offered to buy a box of matches from the foyer kiosk and the lady expressed gratitude.

On my return, we introduced ourselves; her cigarette was successfully lighted and we agreed to remain sitting together for the film. We exchanged standard pleasantries. Her name was Alison and she worked in a bank and she was amused that I was in "the crazy new world of television". Alison was beautifully spoken and I soon became aware that she was well educated, finely dressed and the daughter of a farmer. She could have doubled as a stand-in for Ingrid Bergman. I had discovered my principal lady!

Ingrid Bergman was a leading actress in Sweden before being lured to Hollywood. I first saw her in 1958 as Gladys Aylwood, a missionary, in "The Inn of the Sixth Happiness" and was captured by the exquisiteness she radiated. She may have been born in 1915 but sitting in the dark, in my garden of dreams, following her every movement, seduced by every syllable of her voice, I saw her as a very attractive girl. 1958 was a little early for sexual designs but I longed to meet someone like her, one day, and that day had arrived!

The auditorium's ambient luminance afforded some confirmation of Alison's physical form. She wore a smart jacket and matching skirt, what I termed 'a costume', with fashionable hemline, comfortably revealing the most perfect of knees. The sheen of her stockings caught the reflecting light as she sat cross-legged. Her subtle perfume was Estee Lauder and I was beginning to enjoy her company. I was seven months beyond nineteen but Alison appeared somewhat mature in manner and stature.

With the trailers and advertising films drawing to a close our quiet conversation lowered in readiness for "Tom Jones". We exchanged occasional whispered comments directly related to the film which prompted Alison to reveal her age: she was sixteen but would be seventeen in two weeks' time! My assumption of her maturity had been shattered as I harboured an attraction for mature women but on this occasion the shock was far from disappointing.

From its opening frames, "Tom Jones" promised to be a film of merriment. Its prologue was constructed in the manner of a silent movie with captions and accompanying harpsichord music, in a staccato fashion. The director had used stop-motion and freeze-frames to emphasise dramatic points, stylistic methods of great interest to me. But I avoided impressing or boring Alison with my passion for film production methods.

Tony Richardson, the director, had recently courted public comment. He married the actress, Vanessa Redgrave, the daughter of actors Sir Michael Redgrave and Rachael Kempson, who was playing the squire's wife in Tom Jones. (It was a shrewd move of Richardson getting mother–in-law into his film!) The cast included Dame Edith Evans (1888-1976) one of England's most renowned actresses and Diane Cilento, the wife of Sean Connery from 1962-73.

Alison had been attracted to Tom Jones for her our own reason. But the promotional trailers had courted each of us with "The whole world loves Tom Jones" and we were not disappointed. There was endless adventure and romance.

In bedroom romps we were treated to bare bosoms with cleavages like crevasses, while an erotic feast between the two main characters, just before bedtime, was arresting with every orgasmic mouthful. As the critic had correctly noted, elicited ejaculations came flowing fast!

Alison relished the scene of a deer hunt, a subject close to her heart, she told me. The mounted chase sequence lasted more than six minutes, the result of brilliant film-making and ended in a violent blood spattered scene, tastefully stage-managed. They were the days before anti blood sport protesting so I was unlikely to disagree with my new found company.

I was never too enamoured by the "unspeakable" on horseback, as Oscar Wilde called mounted hunters but on this occasion they were in pursuit of the edible!

Both of us adored "Tom Jones" despite the critic's denouncement. We laughed and chuckled throughout and the cinema for me had been elevated to another level. The story held our attentions for more than two hours and as the end credits appeared I no longer cared what the critic had written. The lights would soon be raised and I prayed they would not cue our closing scene.

On this September day I went out with no thoughts of meeting any girl taking refuge in my 'garden of dreams'. I realised that Alison had changed my plans, with an overriding hope I had been engulfed by love at first sight, without the influence of infatuation.

After the lights went up we were the last patrons to leave the auditorium. We made our way to the spacious circle foyer where daylight poured through the tall windows of the Odeon's facade. Alison may have been barely seventeen but I now saw her as having the classic figure of a mature woman.

By the time we began our descent of the grand staircase I realised there was more to her demeanour. Alison's poise demonstrated a thorough training in deportment, as she coped graciously with stiletto heeled shoes on the marble stairs before making our entrance into the ground floor foyer. I proudly acknowledged a furtive smile from the kiosk attendant who had sold me the matches more than two hours earlier.

We began the long walk to the city centre and my judgement of Alison's mannerisms had been well founded. During our endless chatting she told me her education had been at Lonsdale School, the city's premier establishment for young ladies. With her schooling in the capital and my travelling to work we were at ease with the city.

Much of our conversation centred on the people who crowded its pavements every Saturday. We felt rather superior, simply because the city was ours at this moment and the thoroughfare of Magdalen Street was not a place either of us would normally stroll. The street served its community with a range of shops dedicated to the local populace.

At the fishmongers we stopped for a moment of 'window shopping'. Alison was a shellfish lover, she told me, notably Cromer crabs, still well in season until November. There were a few oysters displayed on the cool marble slab along with cockles and mussels, her other favourites. Alison was fully aware of the nation's obsession with oysters and we talked on the doubtful philosophy of the aphrodisiac while recalling the erotic feast in "Tom Jones". I had never ventured to taste these sensual delights so we agreed this was something for the future. Having just met we were already talking about the future and I had no need for aphrodisiacs!

We weaved our way through the throngs of Saturday shoppers to the departure points for our respective buses home. The bus terminal was at the foot of the grassy mound of the city's Norman castle. With time to spare we decided to take the long climb to the top of this historic stronghold to admire the city skyline and survey the route we had taken. At the summit, the air was suddenly clean. After a while, without words, we ambled to the foot of the castle's towering walls and sat on the nearest bench. Our conversation was over as we moved simultaneously towards an embrace.

Little more than three hours earlier we had never met and now we were engulfed by each other's caressing, oblivious to the occasional passer-by. I was engaging in actions out of kilter for me; a couple in public view heavily petting with hands exploring each other's contours is something I had always viewed dimly.

My memory recalled schooldays when two of my amorous friends were snogging on the edge of the playing field, only to be stopped in their progress by the teacher's whistle. There was nothing but a travel schedule to stop us on this day.

We drew on each other's breath and engaged our tongues in a sensuous duel. Alison's lips were like nectar and as we embraced, my fingers traced the impressions of suspenders though the fine material of her tightly-fitting skirt.

My well-read awareness of a female's workings came into play; that slow process of tumescence, when sexual selection is decided and the crystallisations of love are formed. Our meeting had happened by chance, a mutual attraction, love at first sight, shared passions, chemistry; all things under the canopy of lust.

True love between male and female has to be driven by a modicum of sexual desire was my understanding. I was often told such craving was unconditional to a perfect relation-ship. On this day I disregarded all critics and as we continued to sense each other a new atmosphere engulfed us; the endorphins had signalled playtime and oxytocin, 'the cuddle hormone'.

Our bodies were on course for something we could not bring to fulfilment on this first meeting. We were building to the stage of detumescence, that total conditioning where an orgasm occurs. There was neither time nor place and risked the end of everything if fulfilment had been possible. It was broad daylight, a very public place and it was still 1963!

Like any good film there was a gentle transition to our final scene. We found ourselves back in the traffic at the bus stops with last minute exchanging of telephone numbers and plans to meet at lunchtime the following week. My life was on course for a change of direction and quite proud knowing that I had consensually aroused a female to the point of orgasm.

Alison's bus arrived and we took one last embrace before I saw her safely on board. As the bus disappeared beyond my sight I set my own course for home to take stock of how I had arrived at this stage in life.

Chapter 3

"Please Sir, someone's drawn a cock and balls on James Ayton's board". The entire woodwork class was stunned and I longed that someone would giggle or fart to break the sudden, undisciplined silence. There really was a pencilled sketch of phallic imagery, pointing from the top right-hand corner of my drawing board.

My board had been wiped clean for the start of the lesson so the verbalizer was obviously the artist. Constructing a wooden penis and testicles was not part of the lesson's remit but the pathetically drawn little prick of a phallus and its accompaniments had been sketched to create the biggest embarrassment, like an unwanted erection!

But the class humiliator was unable to expose me as an exponent of erotic art. Had I have been the artist the rendition would have been a perfect vulva, with sensuously pursed lips of labia major and minor, shielding a vaginal opening. At this time in my life I had never seen a real one; I was useless at art and who would have posed for me? The only thing I had ever seen with apparent likeness was a freshly prised oyster with its fleshy sliminess. Furthermore, unlike some of my school friends, I had no sister, so I lacked first hand, up front knowledge.

Erotica, in words or pictures in the 1950's was out of bounds to twelve year olds. But cock was not totally taboo in the English language. Ranging from water main valves to male poultry the noun could be uttered in bona fides statements, until it was associated with accompanying male appendages, where for us, as on this occasion, found itself ejaculated to ceiling level!

The boy who had drawn on my board was incapable of knowing better. He should have known most of my friends were more anxious to see renditions of female genitalia than their own but girls were not in the artist's creative sight that day. He did not understand the word vulva and being too ill educated to use polite language he knew it only as a "fanny". However, his handiwork of a phallic nature was recognisable although its size boasted very little and probably depicted his own pathetic little prick.

Woodwork was taught in a wooden hut, appropriately, half a mile or so from my primary school. It was situated in a narrow leafy lane, almost shadowed by the most important shrine in my life story, the local cinema. For a once weekly escape from the classroom we snaked our way from the main concourse to be taught by our genial master, John Smith, whose pastime was campanology. There was always the latest edition of "The Ringing world" on his desk; the monthly journal for devotees of church bell ringing.

I was nervous as John Smith strode from his podium to inspect the 'eruption' at my workbench. 'Sir' was a man of good substance and while irritated at seeing the sketch, he accepted my side of the story, me being considered a devout sort of boy.

The culprit never owned up although we all knew who it was. He had been loitering near my bench before the lesson but none of us would split on him and now he was in my sights! On Sir's instruction, the art work was quickly rubbed from my board, leaving a look of disappointment on the boy's pale and miserable, hatchet face.

My school at this time separated boys and girls as we had reached teenage years. For most of us sex was a mere blip on the radar although for some, eruptions were beginning to be felt in the trousers! Sex education was not in the curriculum because the powers who governed education decided we had no we need for it and there was not a manual in sight.

In due course, all knowledge was available in the playground where the latest intelligence was passed around. The only "F" word was "frigging" and we began to hear a few girls conversing about whose "time of the month" it was. We heard mysteries of "their cracks" and we longed to see one. Our eyes would strain to catch sight of bulges in gussets of thick blue school knickers under the clothing of senior girls playing netball but the view was obscured by the dividing bit of their sports skirts.

The senior girls were a couple of years older and more developed than females in our age group. Their perspiring physiques when violently dashing around the playground, with "tit wobbles", (bouncing breasts), tussling to get possession of the ball, became a stimulating spectator sport. Daily discussion about what we might achieve if we ever got beyond a gusset was confined to a small group of which I was proudly part.

At this time there was very little fascination for breasts although a few bosoms were beginning to bloom. Sizes varied but they had little significance for us, even though they were very obvious, unlike the concealed, bulging gussets. But somebody would occasionally make reference to "her tits".

As for frigging, there was rumour of a man in the lower end of town who regularly 'frigged' his wife unconscious yet she seemed quite happy! This reliable intelligence came from my classmate John (of 'tit wobbles' quotation fame) who passed the couple's house daily on his way to and from school. He once heard them 'frigging' and we were anxious to know why she was rendered unconscious.

I sneaked my father's war service medical manuals into school on one occasion. He was a medic in the Royal Air Force during wartime and I wanted to enlighten my circle of confidants with descriptions and illustrations of the 'vagina' and 'vulva'. We needed to know what to expect and how to handle one, knowing it was something voluptuous, assuming we would get that far. A concerning side issue in my father's manuals was illustrated descriptions of Crab Lice often found lurking in the pubic hairs, apparently!

As our interest in females grew there were occasional mentions of "their fannies". The word never raised too much excitement for me as I had read of "Fanny by Gaslight" a film melodrama of 1944, the year of my birth. I was becoming fascinated with cinema history because this particular movie's director was Anthony Asquith, the son of Herbert Asquith the one time prime minister. Scenes for Anthony's debut production were filmed on the coast at Cromer, ten miles away and one of my classmates wondered if a fanny would look any different by gaslight, as we still had few gas lamps in the town!

I tried teaching my pals that a fanny's proper name was the vulva, a funnel, rather like an arum lily. And with me having being weaned on the Bible I mentioned the book of Leviticus which brought howls of humiliation. The Holy scribe had laid down laws concerning our subject so we ought to behave ourselves. There were people we could not "lay down with" and let alone the fate awaiting any male or female who might get passionate with an animal! Even our parish church displayed a framed list of people it would not allow us to marry, including our mother-in-law, but this was all too repulsive at our age.

Leviticus tackled the girls' monthly issue too. We had to stay away from them at this time and in any case, none of us had made plans to be with them. One of the brighter Biblical scholars lectured us on the Old Testament, reminding us that this was really the guide for the earliest devout people on earth and did not apply to our group.

We sometimes heard of people "having sex". How did you have sex? To us, sex was what we were, male or female. But we did hear of people who would have a jump, others were having a poke, as well as those we already knew of who were frigging. There was also talk of people having a "bit of the other", an expression for those too embarrassed to say naughty words!

New words joined our vocabulary. Most of us were now getting "the jack", properly known as "an erection" which to us meant putting up a building or monument. It was sometime before we gathered the word derived from "ejaculate" and the "ejaculated" sperm we knew as "spunk", a slang term for semen dating from the sixteenth century.

In traditional language, spunk means courage or pluck but we often attempted to embarrass a teacher by asking them to explain "spunk-water". Disappointingly, we learned it was an ancient term for rainwater; accumulated in the timber hollows at the base of old trees!

As children, we rarely heard talk of sexual issues at home. Our parents never verbalised the topic unless it involved something comical or "smutty". But newspapers sometimes reported shocking stories of young women who had been "interfered with". Such reports made headlines when a female's lifeless and partly naked body had been discovered somewhere off a beaten track, with evidence of sperm on the remnants of her underwear. So did it mean the young woman had been frigged to death?

At this stages in our lives there were no thoughts of romance. There was no big urge to kiss a girl while most boys referred to it as snogging. We had grown to the verge of teenage years understanding that girls were made of something different to us, consisting mainly of "Sugar and Spice and all things nice": unlike boys, who were made of all the offal and stuff along with "Frogs and snails and puppy dog tails", according to a rhyme we had been taught.

We were told to treat girls with care and respect so we often turned our fantasies to a female teacher and one in particular. She was rather young to be our mother but old enough to generate a range of fantasies. There was no consideration as to whether our teacher would welcome us with open legs or any thought that she might reject our advances outright. Assuming it would be all of us, we never got to selecting who would go first, if our fantasy became reality!

I was rather guarded about being the leader although I was excited by the mission. War time RAF bombing exploits were still talked of and I understood that successful raids relied on the pathfinder force going in first. In our case, the first one in would make the way clear for the rest to follow. And just like the heroes in our war stories, get in there quickly, drop the load, pull out safely from the target and head for home without getting caught! That was our idea of what sex involved and we had no thoughts about the outcome if one of us had impregnated our schoolmistress. And little did we know at the time it would have been her fault, in law!

We were heartbroken when her marriage was announced, with suggestions we should contribute to a wedding present. It signalled the end of our fantasy as she would reject us once she had a husband. There was always discussion of whether it really was her or someone else who regularly gave us the "jack".

Sexual intelligence was never discussed at home. We had all been fobbed off with stories of how we arrived in this world; some, like me, had been delivered by a stork! I still have the little card announcing my arrival in 1944 which states; *"The stork has brought us in his rounds a baby boy weighing seven and a half pounds".* We just accepted that the generations before us were permanently conditioned to be embarrassed by the subject.

We were more concerned when hearing that sex could raise its ugly head and we still never understood why it was always dirty? It just added to the thrill and augured well when we began to hear of people having "dirty weekends".

We had ventured into adult territory. In the playground there was dialogue of a new phrase; "French Letters" not mail from France but condoms, rubbers or Johnnies.

Some of us met periodically, out of school hours, in one of the two gent's hairdressing shops in the town. There were no appointments in those days. We piled in and waited our turn, chatting and sniggering; anticipating which man might buy French Letters; ask for something off the top shelf; something for the weekend!

The products were advertised by miniscule, enigmatic plastic signs on the edges of shelves: "Ona Surgical Rubber-wear" at 2/6d (twelve and a half pence in today's currency) for a packet of three! We almost peed ourselves when a customer asked for "toilet rolls", having been aware of a row of waiting boys. By now, we all knew he was not anticipating a whole weekend of wiping his arse!

The Ona brand of condom is unheard of now but the name always conjured intrigue. Modern scholars of translation attribute it to Onan, that minor Biblical character we can read of in the Book of Genesis. He was the second of the three sons of Judah the first born being Er.

Er married a girl called Tamar but he did something wicked in God's sight so the Lord put him to death. This left Tamar 'to be seen after' by her departed husband's family, as was the tradition in those times, and these days it can be best understood from the New International Version of the Holy Bible:

"Then Judah said to Onan, 'Sleep with your brother's wife and fulfil your duty to her as a brother-in-law to raise up offspring for your brother.'

But Onan knew that the child would not be his; so whenever he slept with his brother's wife, he spilled his semen on the ground to avoid providing offspring for his brother.

What he did was wicked in the Lord's sight; so the Lord put him to death also."

It was a harsh punishment for pulling out of the race just short of the finishing post but God forbid masturbating. Semen, generally, although not correctly known as sperm, was sacred and not to be wasted. In recent times the action has been referred to as Onanism, what most scholars on the subject labelled "coitus interruptus". It became a natural method of contraception so the act inspired one rubber company's brand for their condoms; Ona.

But all this knowledge made no preparation for discovering when sex might raise its 'ugly head'. My experience came in the guise of the town's predatory "poofter" and I was caught in his sights for a brief time. He lived in the lane by the school so most of the pupils passed by, twice each day. Although 'poofter' was the applied term, being the only word we knew, it was the wrong label, at that time. The man was really into pederasty, what we term now as paedophilia, a man wanting anal intercourse with a boy. We never heard mention of the word paedophile.

At the age of thirteen I earned money out of school hours as delivery boy for a grocery shop. I pedalled groceries on my trade-bike to customers all over our town with it population of three thousand, which included the local poofter.

Few locals were aware of our resident 'pederast'. Even the townsfolk who thought they knew would not accept it; impressed as they were by his stack of credentials: retired bank manager, upstanding member of the community, living in one to the town's biggest houses, a regular serving churchgoer and he had a wife in tow. To most people, he seemed a perfect gentleman but to wary boys he was a poofter, with ill intents and had been rumbled. We knew of him and the skirts of mother church were hiding him.

When I started my job the grocer alerted me to this particular customer; "He's always after young boys, watch out for him". And he was right. The man turned up at the shop one day, hoping to see me and then came to my home on a later occasion, convincing my mother what a fine gentleman he was. Sadly, she was impressed, but I was already mindful of his constant smirk as he smiled through fine rimmed spectacles over a thin grey moustache as he swaggered, on his way, feminine-fashion, through the town. And I drew the line when he wanted to know if I 'tossed off'.

My employer intervened and proffered a retaliatory plan. He would make all future deliveries to the offender's house, to spare me any dilemma. Unfortunately, the culprit was a marked man. My employer was one of the church wardens and aware of his client's weakness! But sadly, as this current age is witnessing, such occurrences in those days were accepted in ecclesiastical circles and swept under the vestry carpet!

I regaled the discovery of this 'ugly head' of sex to my friends. The man was instantly labelled by one of my classmates as 'a bum-puncher' an ancient colloquial term to describe an active 'bugger', which he once heard his grandfather jokingly mention. Then one of my pals delivered a philosophical bombshell: "This old man might be looking for someone to put a knob up his arse"! There were no volunteers!

In 1957, our egos received a healthier boost. A new dance craze, "Rock 'n Roll", arrived from America promoted through a film, "Rock around the Clock" featuring a pop group, Bill Hayley and the Comets.

Most of us were just a little too young to get swallowed by the fun but it was enjoyable seeing mature girls being swirled around the dance floor. Wide dresses were sent billowing to reveal glimpses of suspenders holding up stockings, giving peeks of knickers, packing in a whole range of gusseted vulvas. A skilled chap could swing his girl in somersault fashion head over heels above his shoulders just to give us a freeze-frame moment with fully revealed thighs and knickers in the air before she came back to earth, along with our dreams.

Something even better than rock 'n roll arrived later the same year. My father contracted to grow a field of low-beans for the local cannery and needed paid pickers so I mustered most of my school friends' mothers, aunts and big sisters. On the allotted day, they arrived mostly skirted and wide dressed ready to bend, squat, kneel or crouch to strip the ripened low-growing crop. Partway through the morning an aroused buzz went around my group to say that someone in the field was not wearing knickers, and she was a big girl! The hubbub never reached my father but he was curiously impressed by the sudden desire of five or six boys volunteering to pick extra beans!

We started working from the opposite end of the rows to meet the other pickers in the middle. Gradual progress through the crop took us to within a few feet of our target and our heart throbbing excitement was confirmed. But all I could see was a region of 'wooliness'; a mat of pubic hair. The rows we harvested in haste had been decimated and word went round that the woman in the field had recently been 'cocked' by someone!

Chapter 4

In September the same year I moved to the local secondary school having failed entrance to the region's grammar establishment. By now, along with my friends, I developed an eagerness for girls as our new regime brought a welcome return to mixed classes.

I began seriously appreciating that some girls were more intriguing than others. A wide variety was bussed in daily from neighbouring villages as the new school served a large catchment area. There were tall and short girls, slim blondes and a few delightful English roses, those generally with a slightly fuller figure. To me, these were the girls who had the makings of real women, with something to embrace; when no one had ever heard the word obese.

My group of pals became more sophisticated and polite as our number reduced to three. We took care with our language, began to show passion towards some of the females, the ones within our class years. The uptake had been split into three levels of assessed achievement for our third year group. I was pleased to be in the highest grade, although I never reached top of the class.

Lunchtimes and breaks provided a chance for friendships to be struck but there was very little serious pairing. But on one memorable occasion a gathering was spotted in the far corner of the playing field, at the edge of woodland, which at first sight was the usual fight. It was not rare, for a lunchtime tussle, but on this occasion there seemed a reason to investigate as it appeared to be rather quieter than normal. A few of us made an orderly stroll towards the crowd.

The encirclement of onlookers surrounded the usual pair on the grass but this was very different. There was no fight but a boy and a girl embracing and rolling around on the ground. Coming as no surprise the girl was Janet, one of those bussed in, and the boy was another of my classmates. The scene was hardly erotic, more like a very friendly scrap, to whatever ends, but we soon had a good idea. One of my friends commented "It's just up her street, knowing her". But I noted differently and informed the uninitiated: "If you look carefully you'll see it's just up her leg, and it's Tony!"

Janet was a shapely girl, lively, agile and in my intelligence group. Sadly, I had been pipped to the finishing line. She was a trifle buxom, strong thighs, broad beam and known for her rosy cheeks, the ones on her face that is. But today they were alight and my comments passed unappreciated!

Tony had the reputation for being able to find his way around. These were the days when girls' uniforms favoured long skirts, and his forearm was out of sight up to his elbow, while they continued their embrace, oblivious of the crowd.

The couple were engaged in erotic fondling or heavy petting as it was often known. It was not unique at our age, about fifteen years, but not as a spectator sport! Tony's face was buried in Janet's breasts, tightly harnessed as they were by her regulation school blouse. I had been aware of the blouse straining at the button holes, causing gaps to afford a peek at the bridge of her expanding bra.

The assembled crowd was relatively orderly apart from occasional calls of encouragement. I suggested to my friends that Tony would soon have to surface for air but their daylight snog suffered a sudden interruptus by the piecing shrill of a teacher's whistle. As we all retreated across the playing field and sauntered back to the classrooms one boy in the throng mumbled: "I wonder if Tony will let anyone smell his fingers?"

I was less adventurous and restricted my occasional fraternising to accompanying a neighbouring girl on the walk home from school. Only the daring walked out of school with a girl as it meant jeering and name-calling the next day: I hated being called Hilary, Elaine or Susie! All three attended Sunday school with me.

Generally, I avoided the class stunners as sometimes they were dismissed as 'prick teasers'. I was drawn to voice and intellect and as school leaving began to loom I put away the coming of age fantasies. I began to think about the future with the ultimate female partner but I suffered one serious handicap: I had been desperately in love with movies since the age of four!

My childhood romance happened one day in 1948 when I was taken to the cinema. At four years old I queued in the rain with my parents to see "Black Beauty", Hollywood's treatment of the novel by a local girl, Anna Sewell, England's celebrated authoress. The film adaption of her novel had taken two years to reach The County, our rural cinema, and everybody wanted to see this film.

Anna Sewell's famous book was published during 1877, the last year of her life. She wrote the story as a narration in the first person; an autobiographical memoir, told by a horse, Black Beauty. Anna's book soon became compulsive reading for Norfolk households, before selling worldwide and making her a local heroine.

In 1948 the publicity told us: "You loved the story. The film is even better". These days, critical scribes dismiss the 1946 production as a "Stilted children's film with little relation to the book". But it did connect itself to the original story, crediting Anna Sewell for its theme and starred two screen notables of the time, Mona Freeman and Richard Denning.

I grizzled throughout the film, as my mother often reminded me, obviously scared out of my mind. But the images registered a curiosity, in particular, a horse-drawn carriage overturning, with its spoked wheel left spinning roulette-like in the foreground.

Getting to the cinema at an early age was a miracle. My paternal ancestors were not enamoured by the new craze of films while my mother had been introduced to them in the age of silent movies, just before 'talkies' arrived. This mixed heritage of my parents created a tug of war where it involved my culture. My father tolerated the cinema if the story was worthy, like his outing to see "Black Beauty".

When the movies were born in 1897 my paternal grandfather was an evangelist of The Wesleyan Reform Union. These non-conformists, with a Puritanical outlook viewed the early cinema as 'the devil's playhouse'. I broke the pattern by falling in love with movies and my school was the maker. Pupils were taken en masse during term time, to the local 'picture house' for special productions, like "The Conquest of Everest" and a record of Queen Elizabeth II's Coronation in 1953. I was hooked by the cinema.

In teenage years, movies became my main source of culture, influencing appreciation of art, music, and literature. It was like going to church: the walk from home and meeting up with others on the way. We paid at the kiosk, filed in, choose a seat in the relevant section and always at the front. We helped swell the 'congregation' to four hundred pairs of eyes focussed on 'the tabs', the stage curtains, waiting for them to part and reveal the screen.

Our best attention was reserved for the 'big film'. Excited applause would erupt from the front rows as the house lights dimmed and the tabs drew back for the last time.

Everyone's gaze was on the screen, except mine! I would strain my neck, turning to view the beam of light from the projection porthole, made evident as cigarette smoke floated upwards to be illuminated. A few years previous, the captivating image of the overturned carriage in "Black Beauty", with its wheel spinning, had shone down this path of light.

The projection room of a cinema was hallowed ground and this one became my shrine. Few people beyond staff or aspiring operators were ever allowed entry. It was noisy, hot and unhealthy, with intense heat from carbon-arc lamps, burning and smelling like a welding shop, with the ever-present risk of a fire!

The cinema was my escape into its 'garden of dreams' to enjoy stories graphically unfolding through fine dialogue with accompanying music. I witnessed real life scenes of national events, some of them tragic, in the weekly Gaumont British Newsreel, long before television. And all this entertainment and education was enjoyed while sitting with girls in the dark!

By the time I was fifteen in 1959 the billboards heralded a ground breaking film was heading my way. "Room at the Top", from the gritty novel of John Braine, was already causing controversy for its treatment of a sexual relationship as a passionate, rather than a procreative experience.

Laurence Harvey, an icon in the making, played opposite French actress Simone Signoret, as the ill-fated mistress, a few years his senior. For young ardent cinema fans, it promoted a boost to the adult world; a young man passionate for the love of an older woman.

The story courted the gradual demise of Victorian morality and traditional class culture of which my generation was now part. It was the kind of film I longed to see but there was just one problem: it was X rated and not for the under sixteens!

I never went to the cinema enough but I read everything available about film production. Room at the Top's star attraction, Lawrence Harvey, was the Lithuanian protégé of brothers James and John Woolf whose Romulus Film company was formed in the year I first went to the cinema. They were legendarily responsible for "The African Queen" 1952 and "Moulin Rouge" 1953, two celebrated titles repeated perennially on television.

John Woolf's name became familiar much later with audiences for "The Day of the Jackal" 1973 and probably the last of the great musicals, "Oliver" 1968. But for me, Woolf surpassed all cinematic milestones in his role as a founder of Anglia Television, the independent television franchise for the East of England who gave me a career.

At school I had been seen as the eternal dreamer and ridiculed because of my passion to work in television. It could never be 'a proper job' I was told; by classmates, teachers and the careers master. To them, the burgeoning television service was reserved for celebrity types so they assumed I would be reading the news! But they were wrong. I was more passionate about sex.

Chapter 5

My first employment after schooling brought the acquaintance of a modern day Casanova. Appropriately, of Italian descent, Frank Mansi loved regaling his exploits to affable audiences and I was eager to learn. He was the wise man who had advised me to meet the mother of any prospective girlfriend.

Frank had amassed a lifetime's experience of women, sampling an array of girls over a range of ages, tasted countless oysters and I became keener for his advice when he revealed a healthy appetite for the older woman. We worked for a traditional home furnisher and I was often assigned as Frank's understudy. Dapper and immaculately dressed, he appeared the perfect lady's man, always resplendent in bow tie. Refined ladies formed the bulk of our customers in this classical emporium, promoted as giving "good service and no discounts". They found their way to Frank's counter of fine furnishing fabrics; everything available at whatever length they desired! Frank had developed an art form of giving good service.

This was 1960 when a lady of "comfortable age" would be offered a seat, while attention was lavished on her. Frank would kneel at the customer's feet, with his sample books spread, fan-like, on the floor; velvets, velours, brocades or folk weaves. She might cross her legs at some point, for comfort, or otherwise; allowing a freeze-frame opportunity to squint beyond her knees and into the unknown. The customer had no idea what was running through Frank's mind and I was keen to observe and learn the skills of the trade. Tights were some way off before ladies were able to discard the stockings and suspenders.

Sexual harassment was unheard of in those days. Today's accused harassers are trapped by their ignorance of wooing skills. Frank wooed every lady customer as though it was a proposal and they loved him for it. They felt safe in his presence as he tripped daintily from woman to pillar to post!

Frank was an archive of carnal memoires. He regaled colleagues with one of his liaisons, a WAAF girl, during the latter part of the war. The service uniform endorsed her figure beyond compare: a tight fitting tunic, restraining firm breasts, a contour hugging skirt and dark seamed stockings, tethered by the celebrated suspenders.

On their first date she just fell into his arms as he caressed the shortest route to her passions and manoeuvred his way under her skirt. Having reached her knickers he soon found she had 'creamed' her gusset; "My knuckle touched it as my hand moved between her thighs and it was sticky" he said: "I knew she'd never been touched". For me, starting out into the world, Frank's related experiences preceded the scripted pages of men's magazines!

Erotic journals had existed for centuries before lining the upper shelves of newsagents in the new age of permissiveness. Two magazines, aptly named "The Pearl" and "The Oyster" were short-lived Victorian publications of underground erotica. They were banned although shoals of erotic writings and illustrations prospered but remained inaccessible to the masses.

Before the sixties, very little advice on sexual techniques had been openly published. There were a few pioneering guides for life, notably for teenagers, stopping legally short of erotica. Museums and galleries held illustrations dating back to the Greeks and works of art by numerous artisans but their renditions were mostly banned from public gaze. Erotica was anywhere but on the open shelves as the law had very dim views on publishing such works.

England was slow to adopt sex manuals. It seemed there was no necessity for us to be shown how to perform in bed, or anywhere else conducive. But a pioneering scientist, Marie Stopes had written and published "Married Love" in 1918. Her sole aim was to help women understand that it was right for them to desire, enjoy and benefit from sexual union without having to bear children. For this, she courted serious opposition.

Marie was born of knowledgeable parents, received a good education and became successful in palaebotany. Far beyond this study of fossilised plants she shew devoted concern for women in problem marriages, having experienced one of her own.

Marie's first marriage was disastrous in that it was never consummated. Her chosen man came into the marriage, quite ill-prepared, and obviously, never came at all! Without total fulfilment she was granted a divorce; such was the law, ruling in a woman's favour. Just as a man expected to get what he desired from his wife, the wife also had her right to receive. Surprisingly, the English had got something right in carnal law.

Stopes found more happiness with Humphrey Roe, her new husband. He had a compatible interest in contraception and went beyond consummation by helping his wife to publish her book which became a valuable guide for many women. Strict rules had governed what was permissible when publishing the subject of sexual actions. Then, long after the birth of the "permissive society" a pioneering doctor with a passion for studying molluscs, including oysters, entered and stole all the attention in the sexual arena.

Dr Alex Comfort (1920-2000) published a boldly produced manual in 1972, "The Joy of Sex: a Gourmet Guide to Lovemaking". It explained everything, for people who knew nothing or for those who knew something but wanted to learn more. Sexual intercourse was presented as a feast, with its designated menu: starters, main courses and deserts! Tucking in from now on became dining out for the passionate.

"The Joy of Sex" was a modern day Kama Sutra. For the English to be able to accept the act of making love as a joy was itself a beauty to behold! This modern guide depicted every satisfying copulating position possible, all consensually demonstrated by a loving, hairy couple, artistically sketched in pen. Pen line illustrations stayed within the permitted bounds of acceptability so we owe much to Alex Comfort's pioneering spirit. Attitude to sex publications had changed.

With the gates to the perfumed garden now permanently open the way was clear to propagate anything sexual. Three years later a pioneering visitor came from America and propagated her own revealing guide: "My Secret Garden: Women's Sexual Fantasies". Nancy Friday (1933-2017) had published this book, her first, two years earlier in America; its success leading to a desperate plea to launch in England.

The author found countless liberated women who wanted to reveal what was really on their mind while their partner was implementing his physical passions. A man might thrive on his own fantasy to achieve his peak of passion but his wife underneath him (unless she was on top, where fantasies can still work!) might be seeing him as a movie star, the man next door, her brother-in-law, a black man, a work colleague, a teenage boy or even a stallion! (And not forgetting the traditional milkman but less popular now since supermarket shopping has driven doorstep dairy deliveries out of business!)

Nancy Friday had tread where other writers had been afraid to set foot. She thought women's secrets had been secret for too long, at least for those who were desperate to talk. She gave the girls a long awaited chance to prove they were far from unusual.

Honourably, Nancy gave men their chance with her next work; "Men in Love" then followed it with it "Women on Top" and "Forbidden Flowers". She brought worldwide awareness for the benefit of men and women alike, to prove it was far healthier to be equally open and free with each other; each to be accepted for what they wished to do.

Fifteen years later, portrayals of female genitalia, emerged blooming in full colour along with male 'danglers'. Sometimes they were stiffly erect in a new hard backed mighty tome: "An Illustrated

Anthology of Erotica". It appeared on bookshop displays in 1992 and soon became the new "pillow book". Erotic engravings from ancient times; drawings and paintings, previously banned from public gaze were revealed with accompanying texts from the delightful works of D H Lawrence and Frank Harris, two of my favourite writers.

Chapter 6

One morning in 2020 I drove ten miles to the public library and waited for the librarian to unlock the door. I was the first visitor on this day of reopening after "lockdown"; a serious national measure taken to combat Covid19, a virulent virus then sweeping the world.

"Good morning. I've come to borrow your copy of "Lady Chatterley's Lover". The branch librarian, who appeared twenty years younger than my children, cast a discriminating glance.

"Oh, that book. It may not be here. We've reduced our stock, to make space, because of the virus".

I returned an innocent smile of acceptance. My hackles rose, restraining my innermost response: "Yes, I know it mentions fucking and cunt a few times, but I intend to read it again after sixty years and if necessary I'll have to buy one of the tatty copies being offered on EBay". I was irritated because I knew the book was in stock.

"The book should be here. I checked the catalogue, on-line, last evening and you have a further twenty eight other copies around the county. I can drive to your next branch, if necessary and pollute more of the atmosphere with my dirty diesel car" was my politely constrained retort.

Planet saving was the last thing on my mind this day. I appreciated the young librarian was dutifully doing her job but I hoped she would understand I was devoted to my subject. After all, this was a library, the book had been published, eventually, and most of the literary world had accepted it.

I elicited the response I wanted: "Of course, you may come in to look but first I'll have to take note of your name and phone number because of the virus". I assumed she accepted I was studying sexual behaviour and did not want my number for a date!

Being an aging memoirist, in my twilight years, I was in no mood for discriminating looks from anyone much younger than my children. Granted an invitation, I could have given her the benefit of my life's experience but on this day I wanted nothing else than to reassess D H Lawrence's masterpiece of English literature.

As expected, I found the book sitting on the shelf, an almost virgin copy, so logged it out to myself on extended loan. Sixty years on from publication in England, "that book" remains an embarrassment to some people.

"Lady Chatterley's Lover", Lawrence's last novel of 1928 was first published privately in Italy, D H's writing location. But the book soon became notorious for its story of the physical and emotional relationship between a working class man and an aristocratic woman but much of the world at the time was unable to accept it.

The work remains an engrossing story of fervent romance. D H Lawrence's aristocrat landowner, Sir Clifford Chatterley, had been paralysed in the First World War leaving him unable to engage in sexual intercourse with Constance, his wife. Chatterley considered his marriage to her so precious that he instigates she gets the "sex thing" from another man.

Sir Clifford is anxious to have an heir to his kingdom so he is happy to promote such a liaison, as long as the resulting offspring can be raised as their own. He would be pleased to have a child running about his stately home and developing the offspring's future providing it never affected Constance's love for him.

D H Lawrence had used a couple of four-letter words, then-unprintable, although they occupied a small portion of the entire text. But it was enough to ban it in England although an expurgated edition was published in 1930

The unexpurgated edition was never released openly in the United Kingdom until 1960. It began with Penguin Books presenting their intended publication to the police. The authorities of England's class-tiered society soon orchestrated an obscenity trial but in the event, the publisher won the lawsuit. In the first year, Penguin sold two million copies of a celebratory edition, dedicated to the twelve jurors who had returned a verdict of "not guilty".

The court case went down in history as a farce. Penguin Books had been accused under the obscene publications act while the defence tackled its case under a recent amendment allowing such publications on literary merits. But it was not just an instance of obscenity by publishing naughty words. Lawrence had highlighted the bedroom secrets of the learned and wealthy, making them very uneasy.

Lady Chatterley engages in a relationship with Mellors, her husband's gamekeeper, the story's principle lover. He lived by his own vernacular and as the narrative unfolds we find him, simply, lovingly, remarking to his new found lady-love what a beautiful cunt she had, and that it was probably the best one left on earth.

Lady Chatterley lacked a full understanding of her own body. Mellors had to give a reasoned description of what he spoke of, hidden under her clothes, although Constance admits to knowing it involved fucking.

The offending words had rarely appeared in such printed form before this time. But the "old guard" were more aghast that Lawrence had suggested such conjugality could be present with a man and woman from opposite ends of the social scale.

Like all Puritan Englishmen at the time, the book's challengers could not cope with anything sexual once it emerged from under the bedclothes and appeared in print. But Lawrence's description of Mellors's first intrusion of Connie's body was hardly offensive for those of sound education:

"She lay quite still, in a kind of sleep, in a sort of dream. Then she quivered as she felt his hand groping softly, yet with queer thwarted clumsiness, among her clothing. Yet the hand knew, too, how to unclothe her where it wanted. He drew down the sheath, slowly, carefully, right down and over her feet. Then with a quiver of exquisite pleasure he touched the warm soft body, and touched her navel for a moment in a kiss. And he had to come into her at once, to enter the peace on earth with her soft quiescent body. It was the moment of pure peace for him, the entry into the body of the woman".

The court case was doomed from the beginning. The prosecutor addressed the jury by asking: "Is it a book that you would even wish your wife or your servants to read?" The result was laughter from the jury with none of them known to employ servants!

The old guard had missed strong points in the story. It was no whimsical tale and went far deeper than sexual liaisons being argued over. Lawrence was aware of a changing world being born out of the mining industry. He saw the aristocratic mine owners enjoying their romance with finance and how it was ruining the environment.

The fleshly story came even closer to the bone with the heroine based on Lady Cynthia Asquith. She was a writer Lawrence had met in 1913 and wife of the second son of H H Asquith, the Prime Minister, whose other son had directed the film "Fanny by Gaslight".

England was ripe for this watershed legal case. D H Lawrence can be applauded for his understanding of the loving, physical connection between man and woman. He considered a woman was in charge while knowing that she had to be wooed by the art of love.

He described Lady Chatterley as having a lithe body; able to reach "her crisis" and hold onto her man after he had "come". She could reach her "crisis", an orgasm, by holding back her own surge, while sapping every drop of her man's ejaculation.

Most people had never heard of D H Lawrence until the trial. It brought to the public gaze a literary work from a brilliant writer whose use of the offending words played a small part in the story.

Fucking and cunt had long been in our language. But the emphasis in court became so intense, when the publisher was cleared, people overwhelmed the bookshops. Their numbers included insatiable young ladies of sound education and literary appreciation; amongst them, I am forever delighted to say, the girl who I married in 1966!

At the time of this trial Alison was in her formal education at Lonsdale, a premier school for young ladies. She was a little more than fourteen when the verdict came through and along with her bevy of turned-on quivering classmates, were "wetting" themselves to get their hands on this novel.

Most of Lonsdale's teenagers were too nervous to visit the bookshops. In the event, Alison was considered more mature and was detailed to go shopping! This was three years before we met, when I had already finished school and was on my career path. After meeting her three years later, I could understand why she had been delegated! Some might have called her a 'big girl' but to me she was classically voluptuous!

Chapter 7

After I discovered Alison in my garden of dreams in September 1963 she never left. That year, we planned to stay together and passed hand in hand, through the exit gate, into "the swinging sixties". Everyone was beginning to rant about "the permissiveness" while our parental generation was straining to cope. But we could see a future laid out for us and decided to play by the rules, or rather appear to, for the benefit of our families.

As a result; "Sexual intercourse began, in nineteen sixty-three. Between the end of the Chatterley ban And the Beatles' fist LP": so wrote the poet Philip Larkin in the opening verse of his memorable "Annus Mirabilis".

For most of his time Larkin was a librarian, who became the best loved poet of our generation, especially when highlighting home truths of British life. Although for him, as he wrote, 1963 came too late, at the same time as the Beatle's first LP; "Please, Please Me"; the very thing Alison and I planned to do!

The Chatterley fiasco was a good start to the nineteen sixties. The upper tiers of the out-of-touch establishment had never explored the floors of humanity's lower levels. It was a heaven sent miracle this work of fiction had liberalised England's cultural landscape so sex was no longer taboo in art and entertainment. The old guard were losing control of the masses and a diminishing belief in God was helping everyone's cause.

But something more than fiction was needed. There was a desire for guidance on the sexual skills in marriage. Not everything came naturally to everybody, after they had walked down the aisle, or even before. In this ground-breaking year of 1963 the wife of a Newark vicar publicly suggested the Church of England should publish such a marital manual.

A request from the wife of a man of the church seemed the perfect prompt. It was perchance the void was partly filled by publication of "The Perfumed Garden", bringing a welcome awakening, albeit from an Arabian, yet Holy passionate perspective. Anyone could now set sail on the orgasmic tide but sadly the course had not been plotted by an English scribe.

"The Perfumed Garden of the Shaykh Nefzawi" a 16th cent Arabic treatise on love was a revelation. I was in London at the time of the book's launching so count myself amongst the earliest buyers. The new translation by Sir Richard Burton (1821-1890) had been banned in England since 1886 until this pioneering year of 1963.

Burton was a British explorer, geographer, translator, writer, soldier, orientalist, cartographer, ethnologist, spy, linguist, poet, fencer, and diplomat; apart from undertaking a translation of The Arabian Nights. He could have been excused for anything he had not achieved in life

The Perfumed Garden was not intended as a "Teach Yourself Sex" manual. It was more a Bible: a guide for perfect living rather than a handbook for couples enjoying sexual union in various positions! It was penned as a celebration of everything that was good, and some things that were not, about the physical union of man and woman. It also proved that our part of the world was centuries behind in providing heavenly tuition to having a good time between the sheets!

1963 became the turning point. We always knew that sex was heaven sent but who decided it was dirty? Most scholars blame The Puritans, that group of sixteenth and seventeenth century revivalists. They wanted to clean up the English church and stop all forms of enjoyment, like theatres and pleasurable romping around under the bed-clothes. They must take credit for creating the "dirty weekend". They maintained physical connection of man and woman should not take place outside of marriage, approved by the church and they started by forcibly cleansing the Church of England from its 'contamination' by Rome.

The Perfumed Garden made no mention of filth. Yet well into twentieth century England, nakedness pictured in books and magazines was still being labelled smutty; in other words, if it promoted sexual delight, it was filthy. The Arabic philosophy of The Perfumed Garden had already made its way to our part of the world since the two hundred years of the Crusades. Much learning in England originated through Latin studies and thoughts and ideas from Arabia with the Koran.

The Greeks and the Romans never had a problem with dirt. When Alison and I were sightseeing amongst the ruins of Pompeii in 1989 we lost count of the number of erect penises, carved in the stonework above the doorways of many houses. There was not a single utterance of filth or muck but we were twenty six years on from 1963!

The tour guide took our party to the house of "Biggus Dickus". He became well known to modern audiences as a fictional character of the Monty Python team. In their film: "Life of Brian", the inspiration for Biggus came from this true Roman nobleman.

On the wall of his restored house was a preserved mural, showing the man with such an extended endowment, in reality, it would have over-balanced him; arse over penis! Just to prove the point, he had been depicted weighing the aforesaid member, perhaps for boasting or Roman tax purposes!

Then, enter the Greeks; they always had a word for it, whatever it was. But when it came to sex they had a way for it, depicted on numerous bits of earthenware. If it seemed possible they had done it, before us and they never thought it mucky!

But while the Puritans were killing our joys the Shaykh Nefzawi had penned The Perfumed Garden. It was "a panegyric of love, a song of sensual delights, a collection of joyous imaginings, a work of rare and curious erotic knowledge"; just the stuff our ancestors would have considered as "filthy"!

Its language form required patience from modern readers in 1964. In the current climate of sexual correctness its scribings might be unacceptable to many but it made blissful reading with its devotion to God for everything displayed by a woman:

"He has furnished her with a rounded belly and a beautiful navel, and with a majestic crupper; and all of these wonders are borne up by the thighs. It is between these latter that God has placed the arena of combat; when the same is provided with ample flesh, it resembles the head of a lion. It is called vulva. Oh! How many men's deaths lie at her door? Amongst them, how many heroes. God has furnished this object with a mouth, a tongue, two lips; it is like the impression of the hoof of the gazelle in the sands of the desert"

Not every man is drawn to a woman's rounded belly but surely, he would not turn up his nose at the sight of a beautiful navel. He might fancy nuzzling in while passionately nosing around. He might have caught sight of her majestic "crupper" (her rear) and what a wonderful thing to hold, or perhaps behold, as it wiggles and sways from side to side as she walks by. These days, in the equine world, it refers to the strap in part of a horse's saddlery, at the rear, but in Arabic, it meant "magnificent buttocks" as round as a mare's!

For sophisticated Englishmen, the vulva has always resembled a freshly prised oyster. It sounded more sensuous than a gazelle's hoof-print in the sand but The Perfumed Garden was centuries before our English perception.

The book's most welcome chapter detailed sundry names given to this organ as we had all been raised to name the vulva and vagina by a variety of profanities. From Burton's translated list of almost forty names I was infatuated by three: *El kelmoune*, The Voluptuous: *El aride*, The Large One and *El menssass*, The Sucker. As translated, these three speak for themselves and were far more appropriate descriptions when compared to fanny, twat, cunt, quim, etc. although the idolatry "pussy" is generally acceptable. English, lesser accomplished writers simply referred to "her sex" which led, ultimately, to "The Perfumed Garden" becoming my preferred reading

Ancient books and their authors had enthralled me from the time I inherited a few tomes of my grandfather's collection. He amassed eight volumes of Blackie's comprehensive "History of England": William Thackeray's "Ballads" and Sir Walter Scott's historical romance, "Kenilworth", published in 1821. The novel, set in 1575, told the story of the secret marriage of the 1st Earl of Leicester and was as close as my grandfather ever came to romantic reading!

Chapter 8

In Victorian times women were sometimes advised to "lay back and think of England". The advice applied at bedtime when husbands were ready and desperate to do their bit. Hannah, like many married women of my mother-in-law's generation, accepted they had to take what came, with little wooing and caressing.

She was often confronted with, "I've got an unruly member" and that was it. She would lay back and never even think of England, accepting that men needed somewhere to shoot their semen. This is what marriage amounted to for so many, but not everybody, and not always. Hannah accepted it as natural while she admitted it could be fun sometimes.

Such a conjugal right was the premise for Marie Stopes' pioneering guide; "Married Love". Hannah was ten years old when it was published but she had never heard of it. The book was not readily available to the masses, particularly to people in rural areas, beyond the reach of bookshops and libraries while not everyone read newspapers. It became a revolutionary tutorial for many wives although the tome had been intended for new and young husbands. Women were pleased to read Marie Stopes advice to men:

"It should be accepted that a man does not woo and win a woman once for all when he marries her: he must woo her before every separate act of coitus; for each act corresponds to a marriage, as the beasts of the field and the fowls of the air know it.

To render a woman ready before uniting with her is not only the merest act of humanity to save her pain, but is of value from the man's point of view, for (unless he is one of those relatively few and diseased variants who delight only in rape) the man gains an immense increase of sensation from the mutuality thus attained"

Hannah was well versed in the physics of reproduction. Like most farmer's children she learnt from an early age that "a hare and a mare take a year"; eleven months of pregnancy for a horse and the balance for the rabbit-like creature! She was fully versed with a human's nine months although her mother, apparently, had experienced a shorter, but 'normal' gestation period.

Hannah arrived barely seven months after marriage, or rather what everyone was led to believe. Babies were always expected to take nine months if they had chance of being born alive. Hannah had harboured the dishonesty all of her life until I was privileged to be enlightened with the truth!

Her father, the young son of a farmer, had engaged in a romantic encounter with a bountifully attractive maid in service to his school friend's wealthy family. The result was a round and fruity house maid, Alice, now minus her virginity and carrying Hannah, the young man's child. In these days of celebrity it would be called a 'love child', an innuendo of this daft period in our evolution! So when is a love child not a love child, especially when born to any couple in love, I always thought, who might also be married?

The parents of Hannah's father were honourable people, not wanting to discredit two notable Norfolk families, let alone shirk their debt to the girl's family. Marriage was agreed so the couple set up home and consigned their story to history until I was privy to the truth of why Hannah was thought to have been a natural 'seventh month baby'!

As an inquisitive, prospective, son-in-law I had made intimate intrusions into Hannah's life. She saw me as an amateur psychologist in sexual matters and I saw her as a worthy subject. But she was always more concerned about getting up at five next morning to milk the cows!

I found her work quite stimulating when talking about warming her hands on a cold morning before handling the teats and pulling and squeezing to get those squirts into the bucket! Thankfully, she had passed the skills to Alison, so I knew I would be in good hands!

By fluke, Alison and I were employed in neighbouring vicinities in our capital city. We could meet each lunchtime and began to be seen together, meeting in the same road at regular times. The comments of my work colleagues came flowing, almost poetically: "She'll kill you; suck you in and blow you out in bubbles!"

My colleagues tended to be less read but meant well. They were ill equipped to deal with voluptuous girls and like my parents' generation were unable to comment on the subject without humiliation. I felt superior with my storage of published advice, ready for those who lacked the relevant education:

"The acme of enjoyment, which is produced by the abundance and impetuous ejaculation of the sperm, depends upon one circumstance, and this is, that the vulva is furnished with a suction pump (orifice of the uterus) which will clasp the virile member, and suck up the sperm with an irresistible force. The member once seized by the orifice, the lover is powerless to retain the sperm, for the orifice will not relax its hold until it has extracted every drop".

I told my friends if they met a girl like this there was no craving for fellatio and scientifically, there could be no reincarnate bubbles! And even if there were, for the benefit of my colleagues' doubt, there was only one response: "Could I wish for a better way to go, floating upwards towards Heaven, in a cloud of bubbles?"

Lunchtime meetings with Alison were easy but weekends involved more organising? We lived some separate distance on opposing sides of the city and relied on public transport; Alison in rural west of the county where her parents farmed and me in a town northwards. Car ownership for the time being was out of the question.

My future in-laws offered the ideal solution: a guest bedroom in their farmhouse was hastily furnished for my weekend stays with a new single divan complimenting tasteful décor. This became my home from home each weekend until well into 1964.

Under the same roof, in adjoining rooms we led a secret life for a few cherished moments each weekend, for many months. Dairy farming meant early rising: cows to be fed and milked so the house was ours for an hour or so from about five in the morning.

Once her parent's footsteps had faded in the yard, Alison would slip silently from her room and the single divan proved wholly adequate. Once more, I was in awe of "Casablanca": "Of all the bedrooms in the house, mine became heaven from the first time she walked in"

On the first occasion, Alison entered wearing a Baby Doll nightdress, a design popularised by a film of the same name. Until this time I had seen her smartly dressed for work only and casually at weekends, generally in ski pants, another popular 1960's fashion. These skin-clinging slacks were tight from the waist downwards, accentuating the full outline of her figure, pulling into every crevice while emphasising the broadness of her beam.

All my imagination was thrown to the wind by her translucent nightdress. I was afforded a diffused view of a perfect mons pubis from the point where her auburn hair was perceptible, suggesting a perfect vulva; what the scribe of The Perfumed Garden called El keuss:

"Such a vulva is very plump and round in every direction, with long lips, grand slit, the edges well divided and symmetrical and rounded; it is soft, seductive, and perfect throughout. It is the most pleasant and no doubt the best of all the different sorts".

The Arabian description was perfect! From the time of my virginal explorations I considered myself well-read but with passion came responsibility. Alison and I were some way from breaking with family protocol, knowing everyone wanted to see us married, eventually, with traditional conventions. As our activities intensified we had to be sure that there would be just the two us, for the foreseeable future!

Contraception had never been a family talking point. Products tended to be sold from under the counter, off a shelf and always out of reach or close to the till. Newsagents, gentlemen's hairdressers and chemists were the obvious outlets but our city had one major benefit, the Norwich Surgical Store.

This dedicated shop was situated in the road where we both worked. From a distance, it was instantly identifiable by the Durex clock, high above the window on the shop's façade, promoting its main product. It was as delightful as a toyshop to a child but here was adult advice and product variety from all corners of the world.

There were numerous concoctions of dubious potency for anxious lovers, trusses to keep hernias in place and embrocations for painful backs. Obviously there were dangers associated with sexual activity!

The pain relieving products shared persuasive, promotional space, with an assortment of condoms, unsurpassed at the likes of gent's hairdressers and Boots the Chemist. Highly attractive were the real skin variety, by the name of Four X, from Australia, nothing like today's synthetic products, but beautifully crafted from animal intestines!

The sensuous sleeve's open end was created with a hem incorporating a rubber band! Preservation of this natural product was vital so the condom was submerged in lubricant, enclosed in a small, capped and airtight plastic container, a little smaller than a matchbox. As with other brands they came in packs of three, but were rather expensive, lacked elasticity and left a chap slipping about like wearing an over-sized fine cardigan!

The contraceptive pill was still quite new. It had been available in the USA first, since 1960 but we were unconvinced of its safety. Then there were assorted barriers for implanting and most burdensome of all; douches, with rubber bulbous ends, like a veteran car horn for a flushing out, rather like a turkey baster! We ruled this out as a 'passion interruptus', being too unmanageable for most of our romantic hideaways.

Immediacy and convenience ruled the day. With stolen moments during weekends, in places like stables, sand dunes, a wine cellar, a variety of woodlands or my 1954 Austin A30 at night but never in the cinema!

There was some laying back, occasional sitting, and even standing but whatever the position, neither of us cared a hoot about England! The reliable products of The London Rubber Company were manageable and reassuring, interspersed with chanced periods of "safety"!

We were a normal couple in love. Had we have 'slipped up', we would have celebrated the outcome, hoping that both sides the family would be pleased. But conception out of wedlock was still a contentious issue, for some classes, and religions, so a quick marriage would have kept everybody happy. We were lucky; engaged, and history records that each of our families had no right to cast a single stone!

Until the year of our meeting, as Philip Larkin had penned, there had been only "A sort of bargaining: A wrangle for a ring". And for me, like many of my peer group it became Larkin's "Unlosable game" as Alison and I entered into a perpetual courtship and spun it out for three years.

On July 2nd 1966 our assembled families wished us well as we left Norfolk in my ancient Austin A30, bound for a honeymoon on the other side of the world; which for us was Bala in North Wales!

"Please be gentle with her", were my mother-in-law's parting, well-intentioned words of plea to me as we set off westerly. Honourably and in good faith I reassured her there was nothing to fear, as I returned a conforming smile, stifling my inner honesty: "Me be gentle with her? Actually, married life began in nineteen sixty-three"!

Alison, and I flowed with the rising tide of permissiveness while never rejecting all marital conventions. The following year of 1967 is celebrated now for giving rise to the "summer of love" and appropriately, it did bring the birth of our first child. While our respective occupations never leant themselves to hippy behaviour, we adopted the new idiom and witnessed the beginnings of changes in social attitudes.

Chapter 9

Orgasm was a foreign word when I began my journey into courtship. I discovered the earliest description of orgasm in Walker's Pronouncing Dictionary of 1848, a Moroccan-bound edition inherited from my grandfather, following his death in 1954. I had faith in words of wisdom when documented by knowledgeable scribes.

"Orgasm: Sudden, vehemence" Walker says, which in turn meant *"Violence or force".* There was no mention of sex, romance, the exchanging of fluids or a state of great satisfaction. The same dictionary posted no entry for penis but it did acknowledge: *"Testicle: an organ of seed in animals".* As for cock, apart from being "a male bird," or something one did with a gun or hat, it could be *"a spout to let out water or any other liquor at will".* But surprisingly, there was: *"Piss: to make water"* and *"Pissabed: a yellow flower growing in the grass"* (Dandelion). During childhood I was told to avoid sniffing dandelions as I would then wet the bed! So despite English modesty, not all words were considered too rude to print!

Walker made no reference to the vulva, clitoris or vagina but he did recognise *"Copulation"* and *"Coitus"* described as *"the congress or embrace of the two sexes".* And not forgetting, *"Impregnate: To fill with young, to make prolifick: fecundation, that which anything is impregnated".* It must have been magic with no details of any happenings between impregnation and the pain of childbirth! The English never came to terms with sex, in narrative and dialogue unless, it was delivered with foul uncouthness or the comical: apart from always being filthy! And I never heard of anybody 'fecundifying' anyone!

Once every delight of courtship came my way, women's orgasms became the subject for discussion. Who was having them and how often: did they 'come' easily and did everybody reach one on every occasion? Until that time the reference had been 'climax'; the older generations had called them 'fulfilments'; to prolific novelist D H Lawrence they were a 'crisis' yet the post-menopausal woman in my story knew only she had "sort of come"!

For most people the art of love developed as a natural skill. The psychologist, Havelock Ellis, considered orgasm controlling as part of "the art" in his 19th century study "The Psychology of Sex" Ellis called it "Coitus reservatus" but D H Lawrence wrote of the action more critically in "Lady Chatterley's Lover". While the story was fictitious the hero's experience of functional women appears familiar to current reality and based, allegedly, on Lawrence's own encounters. His hero, the gamekeeper, proved there were many kinds of loving; as he explains to Lady Chatterley, the recipient of his affection, once she is eager to understand:

"Only to my experience the mass of women are like this: most of them want a man, but don't want the sex, but they put up with it, as part of the bargain. The more old-fashioned sort just lie there like nothing and let you go ahead. They don't mind afterwards: then they like you. But the actual thing itself is nothing to them, a bit distasteful. And most men like it that way. I hate it. But the sly sort of woman who are like that pretend they're not. They pretend they're passionate and have thrills. But it's all cockaloopy. They make it up. Then there's the ones that love everything, every kind of feeling and cuddling and going off, every kind except the natural one. They always make you go off when you're not in the only place you should be, when you go off. Then there's the hard sort that are the devil to bring off at all, and bring themselves off, like my wife"

Lawrence had pre-empted most of women's orgastic reactions in one paragraph. He had experienced all types ranging from the fake orgasm to the girl who could never wait for her man to bring her to a climax.

There was often talk of women faking orgasms. Other people's bedroom encounters will always excite somebody: therein lies the premise of erotica and pornography. But women pretending to be reacting to this most ultimate of female achievements seems rather sad: even sadder if her partner is satisfactorily convinced by the display. As well-versed couples know, yelled utterings alone are unconvincing. Screams of "Yes" and extolling the virtues of Almighty God belong to the scripting's of dramatic enactments!

A dexterous woman might be able to induce voluntary spasms in her vagina. It requires something extra to persuade the orgastic lock-gates to open, releasing that confirming stream, oozing around the mouth of the vagina. Real tears of ecstasy are known to follow, in some cases, giving a natural opportunity for the man to caress his partner to recovery. This is a real orgasm, although the occasional, simultaneous, involuntary emptying of the bladder might dampen the ardour!

Meanwhile, commercial film dramatisations have immortalised the orgasm. Much talked of in recent years was portrayed in a film; "When Harry Met Sally". The production of 1989, from the novel by Nora Ephron, concerns a young couple who meet occasionally over a period of twelve years. They discuss whether there can be a lasting friendship between man and woman without an active sexual fixture.

Meg Ryan and Billy Crystal were the lead players and one of their meetings became rather heated at a restaurant table. During the feast our heroine tests her friend's ability to know whether he would really appreciate when his partner might be in full orgasm, although the "O" word is never uttered! Meg Ryan, as Sally, enters into a trance-like vocal demonstration of the comprehensive works, just to prove that Harry would not be able to appreciate the difference between real or fake.

Most of the diners are convinced that Sally has orgasmed during mealtime. A middle aged lady, dining close by, summons the waiter to order: "I'll have what's she's having". Meanwhile, Sally exits her eruption, re-joins the conversation as though nothing had happened, leaving Harry looking embarrassed, totally fooled and open-mouthed.

As a classic romantic comedy "Harry met Sally" passed through the cinema with its noisily demonstrated orgasm, without causing offence. But fifty five years earlier, audiences were unprepared for dramatically demonstrated erotica, albeit virtually silent.

In 1933 a Czech film, "Ecstasy", crossed the border lines of the law. In those days, the title described pure bliss and not a pill for popping at parties! The story told of Eva, a young woman who marries a rich older man before discovering he is obsessed with a life of order. Finding he has no room for passion, Eva becomes despondent and leaves him, returning to her father's house. One day, while bathing in a lake, she meets a young man and they fall in love. Meanwhile, the husband has become grief stricken at the loss of his young bride, and fate brings him together with the young lover that has taken Eva from him.

What seemed an innocent story of romance caused a furore. Eva had slipped sensually nude into the lake for a swim and on emerging from the water displayed her wholesome breasts along with the rest of herself. Totally naked, she runs through woodland, attempting to capture the horse which has galloped away with her clothes. A young man in the vicinity joins the chase and apprehends the animal, triggering a thankful Eva to enlist the fellow as her new lover. An ecstatic display in the subsequent bedroom scene with Eva's convincing orgasm was more than most of the world could take. Since the birth of film censorship in 1913, the censors had waited in the wings to ban such scenes.

The enactment by a young woman discovering and expressing sexual pleasure in extreme close-up, on her face, was considered too pornographic for public distribution. The film was part silent but the agonisingly passionate expressions of her face, while being caressed by her lover and a close-up of her hand releasing its hold on a string of pearls, suggesting the peak of orgasm, was more than the censors could accept. Yet the whole sequence was silent!

Germany banned the film outright while other countries made harsh cuts before allowing it to be shown. But uncut copies found their way to America where the young Czech star, Hedwig Keisler was later enticed to Hollywood and renamed Hedy Lamarr. Today's audience would find the visuals tame and stilted but Hedy Lamarr was now tagged the "most beautiful girl in the world" and everybody knew why!

D H Lawrence wrote of Lady Chatterley's "crisis" (her orgasm) when she engaged with Michaelis an occasional visiting lover who had befriended her husband. Michaelis was an Irish playwright and part of Sir Clifford's circle of friends but Constance secured him for something very different:

"He was a more excited lover that night, with his strange, small boy's frail nakedness. Connie found it impossible to come to her crisis before he had really finished his. And he roused a certain craving passion in her, with his little boy's nakedness and softness; she had to go on after he had finished, in the wild tumult and heaving of her loins, while he heroically kept himself up, and present in her, with all his will and self-offering, till she brought about her own crisis, with weird little cries".

Those "weird little cries" were familiar to Frank Harris, the second of my literary heroes. He wrote about sex quite poetically, adorably and explicitly; without uncouthness, in his published memoirs of the women he loved and referred to the female orgasm as a state of hysteria.

Irish born Harris (1855-1931) emigrated to the United States early in life. He read law at the University of Kansas, became bored by the legal profession and returned to Europe in 1882, settling in London to pursue a career in journalism. In 1921 he took US citizenship and attracted much attention during his life for his aggressive personality and editorship of famous periodicals while befriending the talented and famous.

Harris's multiple-volume biography "My Life and Loves"; was banned in countries around the world for its sexual explicitness but luckily for educated folk, not forever! One of his loves was a pretty girl called Lorna:

"She kissed me hotly, foraging and thrusting her tongue into my mouth. Finally she pulled up her chemise to get me further into her and at length with little sobs she suddenly got hysterical and panting wildly, burst into a storm of tears.

That stopped me: I withdrew my sex and took her in my arms and kissed her; at first she clung to me with choking sighs and streaming eyes, but as soon as she had won a little control, I went to the toilette and brought her a sponge of cold water and bathed her face and gave her some water to drink—that quieted her".

Frank Harris had introduced his readers to the sexually related hysteria, "a wild uncontrollable emotion or excitement", in other words, an orgasm. It was a condition known to be associated with the female of our species; or so we were led to believe.

Historically, beyond the vows and the marriage bed, hysteria was treated as a disease of the mind, deeply rooted in the womb. It affected many young women and often was labelled the 'widow's disease'.

Havelock Ellis found there had been a tendency to exaggerate the character of the auto-erotic sensations of hysteria. He considered this was the inevitable reaction against an earlier view, according to which hysteria was little more than an unconscious expression of the sexual emotions. In other words, Ellis was telling us that it was part of a woman's make-up to be hysterical, and it was not really a problem but rather it was an orgasm!

Today's women and medical science no longer accept the historical diagnosis of female hysteria. As a disease of the mind it was consigned to history although its legacy, hysterectomy, remains in place. The vital surgical procedure for removal of a diseased uterus is often a lifesaver for some women when threatened by the condition.

But there is a positive excitement with female hysteria. The word rhymes romantically with wisteria, that twining vine with attractive pendulous flowers, signifying 'over passionate love' and 'obsession'. Having descended from a long line of gardeners, I knew wisteria required sturdy support and regular pruning to keep it under control. But unlike hysteria, the wisteria contains toxins, liable to cause anything from nausea to death, so my guide in life has been to sample no more than I could savour at one mouthful!

Chapter 10

My mother-in-law was predisposed to the attitude that women in marriage were abused and treated as doormats. Hannah held serious Christian beliefs but disagreed with the wedding ceremony's vow to 'obey' yet she chose to wed. I was often reminded of her obsession that all men were stallions so I chanced an assumption she harboured frustrations.

She was always concerned for Alison's well-being, just as mothers would be, once marriage was in the offering. She reckoned people loved "getting babies" but were not always capable of raising them correctly so I faced her challenges like a true son-in-law. She often told me I was different although my wife had already told me the same; because I was "over sexed", apparently! I still have no idea of what over-sexed means.

I continually envisaged Hannah as Alison in years to come. They were comparable in physique and mannerisms at the time we first met, despite Hannah's fifty five years to Alison's seventeen. But times had moved on and while Hannah was my mother-in-law of some fifteen years she was now widowed.

While single, Hannah Keeler had lived a chaste life, barring her intended husband from "touching" until they were married. After a long courtship of some thirteen years her man informed her he would wait no longer: "It's now or never", so they cycled to the registry office at 0830 one foggy winter's morning for a legally binding marriage, witnessed by two friends.

Hannah's prudery was often questionable. I remembered one occasion when her husband was talking about shellfish and teasingly reminded her of why men loved savouring oysters. He took the brunt of one of her serious but embarrassed rebukes in return, giving me a confirming insight to all I had thought; proof of her perception of all things sexual.

Hannah had been scornful of the 1960's, constantly dismissing much of the new wave as "bum-holes" (a colloquial for nonsense). My generation was dealing with the new freedom but conception out of wedlock had coloured Hannah's opinions of all things sexual. She had lived a lie, through no fault of her own, conceived out of wedlock, born into a family of upstanding people who would never admit to 'getting caught' having committed a 'dirty sin'!

She regaled me with stories of men she had encountered, like her brother-in-law, who insisted the answer to most women's ills was "a good poke" and a visiting farm rep who reputedly had "poked the life out of his wife!"

From the time we first met Hannah had opinions of what lie ahead for Alison but she did accept my philosophy was different. I chanced she could not read my mind and smiled in agreement at her sermonising while stifling my inner-most response: "But your daughter is like you, strong willed, and you are jealous. I wonder how many times you reached fulfilment in your own marriage and could you orgasm now: I reckon you could. Given the chance I could prove it"

An age gap relationship was a timely subject for the cinema in 1967. In the year history records as "the summer of love", Dustin Hoffman and Anne Bancroft performed in "The Graduate". The film was deemed fitting for the anything-goes mood of the late nineteen sixties; titillation, lush filming, excellent performances and music by the popular duo, Simon and Garfunkel.

The story unfolded of a young man, fresh out of college, who is seduced and given the best initiation for life by Mrs Robinson, the wife of his father's best friend. But once set up with a whole bedtime of experience he chooses to walk off into the sunset, with the Robinson's daughter, much to everyone's relief!

It was a rare topic for the cinema. It was my subject and even better when the next story came along; again, from America. This time it was a dark comedy which one critic called "the epitome of bad taste". Such was "Harold and Maude" in 1971 but I found it amusingly touching and entertaining. Harold met Maude at a funeral. Individually, they had gone to the committal of a total stranger but discovered they had a shared interest: a fixation with death and attending funerals.

At home, Harold was forever acting out theatrical suicide attempts, to draw the attention of his dismissive, social climbing, mother and Maude came to his rescue. They embarked on a romantic journey with Maude giving Harold a fresh outlook on life with a real zest for living.

It appeared a classic romance; a repressed young man meets an astonishing woman. They share interests, have endless fun, fall in love, make love, and arrange to marry but the young man's chosen bride commits suicide just before the wedding. How sad, it could be said, for a young man in his early twenties but then you must know that his dream girl was seventy-nine years of age!

"Variety" magazine reckoned the film displayed "all the fun and gaiety of a burning orphanage". It took time for cinemagoers to accept it, show appreciation and more years than usual for the production to make financial returns. But music from Cat Stevens, known to us now as Yusuf/Cat Stevens, helped it to achieve cult movie status. Finally, it occupied a creditable number forty-five in the list of America's top one-hundred comedies.

The film's casting was unsurpassed. Bud Cort, as Harold, was then twenty-one and already known for playing boyish characters. Ruth Gordon (1896-1985), seventy-five years old at the time, was the ideal Maude.

Despite society's new freedom on both sides of the Atlantic, film lovers found it uneasy. The theatrical suicide attempts were more or less accepted but the romantic relationship was more than most folk to take, and how sadly hypocritical. But at least the producers had discovered the public's sexual Achilles' heel!

To ardent Christian believers, sexual union remains sacred for procreation. Had the roles been reversed, with Maude as a menopausal twenty-one year old model or pop-star and Harold, a wealthy old business magnate, the audience would have queued to spur them into action. "Hasn't he done well?" they would have yelled and then counted the months away to see the proven fruits of his labours, or rather, his wife in labour!

A wide age gap between a couple mutually attracted is not unknown. History is strewn with old men taking young wives, at every level of society. Generally, the young wife is well within childbearing age, like my mother who was sixteen years younger than my father. But if the roles are reversed a new set of critical guidelines come into play.

Hannah was seventy-six in 1984 and I was forty. While she saw it inevitable that a young man may not want to love an old woman she saw no reason why old men with young wives should have all the fun. The very subject had fascinated me from schooldays so I was turned over and captivated by her response.

Beyond Hannah's opinionated assertiveness there was often a sparkle in her eyes. I never took fright of her dispatching of males, considering myself neither brutish or useless and certainly not endowed as a stallion! In today's parlance she had caused a 'blip on my radar', but I recalled the scribe of "The Perfumed Garden" warning against involvement with a much older woman:

"Be on your guard and shun coition with an old woman; in her bosom she bears the poison of the arakime. A proverb says also, 'Do not serve an old woman even if she offered to feed you with semolina and almond bread'"

Coition or coitus, from the Latin, was a medieval term for sexual intercourse. Arakime, the plural of arkeum, was a hideous serpent with a fatal sting and the notion of Hannah's breasts concealing the poison of a snake I could ignore. She may have possessed firm, ample breasts but my appetite would have shunned semolina and almond bread! As a child, I never warmed to semolina pudding!

Hannah was quite akin with marriage age gaps. Her late husband was eight years her senior and another family member had married someone old enough to be his mother! The subject became an early conversation piece and I introduced her to a key passage in the "The Perfumed Garden" as she was fascinated by my obsession with books:

"Know that the man who works a woman younger than he is himself acquires new vigour; if she is of the same age as his he will derive no advantage from it; and, finally, if it is a woman older than himself she will take all his strength out of him for herself"

Her hair might be grey, her body no longer lithe but signs of old age were no proof of what lay dormant and yearning in her mind. Had she orgasmed throughout married life? The elation of being able to satisfy a very mature woman, knowing that she had been attracted to a young man, would set the right forces in motion.

My way to her seemed clear. Hannah was generally supportive of me and admired my life's achievements but we could come to verbal blows on occasions, if I stirred her wrath. I was still analysing and estimating her, seeing her as Alison in later years. By now, I knew she needed to be pacified so I set my course to woo her.

Chapter 11

Hannah's attitudes toward marriage had intrigued me from our first encounter. She had convinced would-be suitors she was worth the wait and her eventual choice of husband, son of a neighbouring farmer, was an equal match. But her parents had delusions for something grander although Hannah's choice was way above the gamekeeper of Lady Chatterley!

Her chosen man had been conditioned to a thirteen year courtship, with no physical intimacy until they wed. They married in 1944, the year I was born, but only after he gave her an ultimatum; it was then or never. Surrendering her virginity at the age of thirty six was rather late but it was her choice.

Hannah's subsequent conception occurred late in life. Giving birth to Alison had been painful, resulting in a near death situation for mother and child, leading to a long recovery and convalescence.

Alison's strong constitution was attributed to her delivery by Caesarean section. According to Hannah, babies born this way conserved all their energy in "getting here without force" she often reminded me. It was a strong belief at the time; although often dismissed as an 'old wives tale' these days but the theory is worth considering.

After giving birth, Hannah was advised against having more children, suggesting further conception was still possible. This made me sympathetic to her opinions of men in general but I let my intrigue become a fantasy.

Could an aging post-menopausal woman still enjoy sexual intercourse and for how many years? I often wondered if Hannah was still capable of achieving an orgasm, assuming she had orgasmed, as some women claim never to have climaxed.

With my peer group, I had grown up in the knowledge that old women "dried up" and older people "going at it" was disgusting. But I realised most of my inherited knowledge of sexual practices lacked substance, confirmed by my bibliographical studies.

Hannah would often come to my aid in family contentions. There were occasional criticisms and opinions of me from her extended clan. Apparently, I was somebody who had infiltrated the family's rural respectability with my improper profession, shoulder rubbing with graduates, budding debutantes, the daughter of a circuit judge and men wearing make-up (announcers and actors). To top it all, I had never graduated and that was a heinous crime!

Hannah was quick to defend me and I rather enjoyed the attention, respecting her in return.

By the time I was thirty five Hannah was double my age. She had been widowed for a year, and left totally alone in the world apart from Alison and our two children. For better or worse, after much consideration, we moved home to a large house and took her under our roof.

Our lifestyle brought a steady stream of visitors, whose company Hannah would enjoy. We engaged a variety of social rounds through my work in television; Alison in her world of commerce, while both of us were involved in local politics. Most villagers knew us. We were busy 'thirty somethings' and Hannah was never without meeting pleasant people. But she often objected to Alison's female friends who she considered to be 'ripe women'. In plain language, women about my age, coming into the house!

Being the only man in Hannah's life I sensed a degree of jealousy. Widowhood had robbed her marital sustenance but she often showed signs of a rekindling, always enjoying a man's conversation. Hannah would listen and engage intently with any subject I discussed. As a result, I drifted and trawled the depths of my imagination until I began to imagine how congenial sexual intercourse might be with her. For me, such an act would be more a connection with history.

It was the most delicate period in my life. From the time Alison and I met I had mostly ignored their occasional mother daughter clashes, uneasy at times, and it had always been historically challenging from what I gleaned. But now, sharing the same home may have been a mistake so it had to be dealt with.

Alison and I had built our life on her business logic and my creative spirit. The only break from the pressures piled on her was our annual holiday. Hannah took pride in housesitting while we flew off on foreign holidays and the break was good for all of us. In August 1987, we took our first trip to the southern coast of Italy, staying in the old town of Amalfi. It was memorable for the breath taking scenery along the Sorrentine Peninsular.

In glorious weather Alison was enjoying the break of her lifetime. She loved foreign holidays and perhaps sometimes pushed the limits of her endurance. But on this occasion, nature overruled and she collapsed. Immediate attention enabled a temporary recovery but thorough investigation was advised on our return to England. An urgent diagnosis found an advanced uterine disorder; the need for a hysterectomy. Life seemed so unkind, sometimes. Was this the price of motherhood?

Alison was placed under the care of a skilled consultant. But having to abstain from our sexual activity for the critical healing period, she was convinced I would never cope. Her stoicism took control with a solution which shook me to the core. She suggested her mother become my surrogate partner, for the duration of the healing!

But Alison had ulterior motives. After admitting and concealing awareness of her mother's passion for me she wanted her to be 'hurt' by this sudden opportune natural act of retribution.

"I just want you to take her. That's what she always wanted. I'll know where you are and you'll hardly know the difference. She was smitten by you from the start and so was her sister. She was jealous each time I fell pregnant. It was proof I was getting what she wanted. Give it to her; fuck her! Take her whenever it's convenient. You'll find her like a virgin. She's well-formed 'down there' and almost hairless. She was never stretched at my birth. After that, she never let my father have much but she still wanted it! She should be able to accommodate you. Exhaust her!"

Alison's forthright lyrical orgasm was unprecedented. This was her fantasy and tantamount to her own arousal. Her mother had controlled her for much of her life and this was a chance to pay back with me as a lamb to the slaughter. Most of all, my own fantasy was about to be fulfilled but for a moment my bluff might have called.

Alison reasoned with her mother and she was anxiously willing. She was flattered to think that I should want to waken dormant sexual desires of an old woman, long abandoned since widowhood. I would be playing a mind game because deep down I knew she always wanted me while she was unaware of my fantasies, or so I thought.

A young man and a very mature woman engaging in the ultimate of physical relationship would garner disapproval from any quarter. But I was Hannah's son-in-law with a bona fide excuse without being guilty of adultery and I was forearmed with the philosophies of Marie Stopes. Mature, healthy and intelligent women from Hannah's era were known to harbour desires for the physical connection resulting in a fulfilment while at the same time being indoctrinated it was wrong.

The initiation of this surrogacy happened early one morning. Being first to wake in the household I generally made the early morning tea and Hannah was already awake when I delivered her cup. With the tea I planted a passionate kiss on her forehead. She responded by removing my left hand from her shoulder and dragged it under the bedclothes thrusting it between her thighs, saying; "That's where you want to be".

Immediately, I felt the warmth of a fleshy mons pubis, like a small cushion, through her nightdress. What I had assumed over the years was now wholly proven but this morning was hardly the place and time.

Her impatience was my immediate reward in knowing I had stimulated her quiescent desires. We agreed it would be unwise and impossible as the rest of the household would soon be rousing but an opportune time was sure to present itself. She told me I was only the second man in her life to have put his hands under her clothing although a few others had hinted intentions. And of the few who tried, they had narrowly escaped to tell the tale, having decided to avoid 'a crack over the skull'!

One quiet afternoon I was allowed to explore Hannah's respected region without sustaining injury. Nothing could have been more convenient than the weekly changing of bed linen and she was often glad of help. Once the freshly laundered bed linen were in place, caressing came easy and our age gap was no hindrance. As we progressed, she nervously suggested there was something wrong 'down there'. The intrigue of her comment was tantamount to arousal.

Hannah dropped back on the bed and I explored under her clothes. Stockings and suspenders I had glimpsed in earlier years were no longer evident, replaced now by thick support tights. Tights entered the fashion scene with the mini skirt of the nineteen sixties. She had never worn a 'pelmet', her name for the mini skirt, but she welcomed tights as a better option than fiddling with suspenders every morning.

Traditional cotton knickers and tights were now layered up to her waist; over a sturdy girdle with a strong gusset hooked tightly in place covering her vulva. It was like a chastity belt. Such variety of under apparel could have been passion killing but for Hannah, a dormant yearning appeared to show signs of erupting, like an extinct volcano.

Sensuality was present, even through layers of clothing. By the time I reached the top she clinched my hand between her thighs, just short of the gusset. Hannah drew back her skirt and insisted I remove her tights then the undergarments by unclipping the girdle's gusset to make access easier. I was in no hurry but she became impatient.

After fumbling with fasteners I revealed her "Mound of Venus". To be a little less romantic and give its Latin description, Mons Pubis, the inverted triangular pillow of fleshy tissue, at the lower end of a woman's abdomen, where the hairs grow, pointing downwards, forming an integral part of the vulva. A mature mound can provide a rewarding handful for the explorative lover as it harbours glands and erogenous components, contributing to successful orgasms.

I exposed a sensuous, almost hairless, vulva. The labial lips had fallen free from the compaction of her tight fitting girdle, revealing faultless genitalia of dark pigmentation. Contrary to old beliefs her labium was not 'all dried up', had the same texture of Alison's but slightly smaller.

Despite her pre-warning of something amiss I could find nothing wrong. Her vulva was firm although little further under her crotch, towards the rear, which explained why I had noticed the impression whenever she was stooping. Her pubic region was dense and probably developed through years of cycling, a condition not uncommon in some women. But during pregnancy the midwife had told her there was something not quite right.

For most of her younger life, when strong and agile, Hannah had cycled miles in the days before her father owned a car. She had told me discomfort was often present after cycling. The pounding of her pubic region, on a saddle not designed for the contours of a sensuous vulva, caused nature to make amends. Modern female cyclists have been catered for, with accommodating saddles, especially those professionally participating in sport.

The skin of Hannah's thighs was smooth, unlike the scaly surface of her shins and calves. They bore the weathering of years of exposure to heavy farm work. Yet her thighs were healthily shapely for their aging years.

She encouraged my gentle caressing upwards to where she knew I wanted to be. Having parted her labia to explore the vaginal entrance I found and touched her clitoris, gently applying a salivary finger. Hannah's breathing quickened to little gasps. In a very short time she murmured; "You've found the spot", followed almost incoherently with; "Put some fingers in"!

I did as commanded, gently inserting my index finger while stimulating her clitoris with my thumb. I kept manipulations slow and engaged her in quiet conversation. She claimed never to have touched herself there and never knew "the spot's" real name. She had always known it to be a most sensitive area but insisted she had never masturbated. This, the ultimate of experiences, meant I had wooed an almost unsullied seventy six year old, who had conceived and given birth to the girl I married.

Hannah's constricting vagina seemed comfortable with one finger. It was understandable considering her age and having been without sexual incursion for eighteen years. With her only child delivered by Caesarean section, stretching through normal delivery had never occurred. But nature was in our favour as I felt the first muscular convulsion of her vagina and she repeated her plea for more fingers while I felt her clitoris swell slightly and she began naturally secreting.

Gradually, her vagina accepted my index and middle fingers. While realising her capacity was just short of virginal my absolute thrill was in bringing this seventy six year old to orgasm. This very real orgasm caused her to be loosened from our embrace as her legs stretched rigidly and breathing became deeper making coherent speech impossible for her.

By now, the muscles of her vagina were keeping my fingers captive. Before long, she gave one last sigh and a sudden emission allowed a slippery exit. I had reached my pinnacle of achievement proving nonsense of the long held theory that much older women dried up! Hannah had truly orgasmed, gasping in silence!

In Hannah's younger days it was termed a fulfilment. Her sudden kindness, like her secretions, were now flowing and she suggested I should enter her for my own relief. I needed no encouragement knowing I could delay ejaculation no longer. Full intercourse with her involved a little repositioning as her bulging belly had never regained its normal shape after giving birth but it mattered nothing.

I took my weight on my arms and she took my erection in hand, guiding me to her labial lips. Once there, the sensation was so sensitive that my semen issued spontaneously before I could attempt entry. It was neither failure nor disappointment as penetration at our first encounter would have caused Hannah some discomfort. During our relaxed conversation we talked of the pleasure there might be in the days ahead, in working at dilation.

We were both at the start of a journey. Hannah was catching up on times lost and I was about to tread a hallowed pathway. She claimed to have known the very night she conceived her daughter early in 1946 when her husband's semen "shot to the top"! She suggested my erection was bigger than his but she hoped to take it in due course!

I complimented her response and my reward in being able to bring her to fulfilment. With a dismissive chuckle she simply retorted; "You just found out you didn't know me and you can't kill an old brier". I trusted she had not just laid back in the hopes of taking 'an unruly member'.

Hannah's "old brier" adage had been handed down for generations. Brier, colloquial for plants of the rose family, can die down, be trimmed and left for dead only to return and blossom in the fullness of spring. With the correct handling, just as Mary Stopes advised, Hannah had regenerated a yearning to bloom again:

"Where the two are perfectly adjusted, the woman simultaneously reaches the crisis of nervous reactions and the muscular convulsions similar to his. This mutual orgasm is extremely important, but in

distressingly many cases the man's climax comes so swiftly the woman's reactions are not nearly ready, and she is left without it"

Hannah had made it first so had not been left wanting. I was proud to have compromised Marie Stopes' advice by bringing Hannah to climax ahead of me. She was aware she had "sort of come", but at the same time, embarrassed that she had "come on" so quickly, in the first instance. Apparently, in her young days, it was not the accepted thing, which is why Stopes set out to make women better informed and not to feel guilty for their inner desires.

Hannah was now relaxed beyond compare and accepted nothing was wrong 'down there'. She had always been a strong believer in the after-life although insisted her late husband had no further need for her now and I was at liberty to take whatever I wanted of her. Everything had unfolded as nature intended and I hoped our encounters would continue through her desire rather than duty.

Chapter 12

My liaisons with Hannah were opportunely infrequent. She likened me to "an old king" with more than one wife and occasionally I was oblivious to which bed I was occupying. I developed a routine whereby I could caress Hannah into an orgasmic slumber before returning to my own bed.

Alison was content, realising her mother was under control and I was gratified. Meanwhile, the consultant suggested physical activities could safely resume between Alison and myself, with care and gentleness. At this point Alison stoically announced; "You'd better start feasting on oysters if you hope to continue keeping the two of us satisfied!"

At around four every morning Hannah had need to visit the bathroom. Being a light sleeper, I was often aware when she crossed the landing and subsequently conscious of her return, with the quiet closing of her bedroom door. One day I suggested she might leave the door ajar, if she desired my attention. Alison agreed to my plan, provided I return to our bed before the house began rousing.

The night before the first occasion was likely to present itself I set my alarm to four-am. There was always a chance that I might miss Hannah's movement. Four o'clock came and went and my pulse began to quicken while I listened intently for footsteps on the landing. I had to accept her call of nature might vary on occasions but within about twenty minutes my chance arrived.

When the bathroom door closed I put on my dressing gown and moved silently to Hannah's bedroom. Before she returned I disrobed and climbed into the vacant side of her double bed. I risked she might react in surprise but the shock, surprisingly, was mine.

In the dim light she saw I was there and climbed back into bed, as though I had never been absent. With only her nightdress between us she said I felt cold and pulled me close to take her warmth which I accepted and prepared myself to take much more.

For the first time, after rolling up her nightdress we experienced each other's total nakedness. As my hands assessed her torso I discovered her breasts were somewhat firm. I suckled on her small nipples, in the hope of drawing them proud and she told me, apologetically, that none of her maternal line had been well-endowed. But Hannah had no cause to be ashamed. I had lived to tell this tale; her breasts made adequate handfuls and did not bear "the poison of the arakime" as the scribe had warned!

We embraced and clung to each other like husband and wife. My hands slid upwards of her soft thighs and parted once more the labium lips to torment her clitoris while she clasped my erection.

I slowed her fondling of me as involuntary secretions were lubricating the palm of her hand and giving me increased excitement, which would have meant an early ejaculation. I had to prolong the act as far as possible so I engaged her in whispered conversation while I continued fondling her.

Hannah's openness for conversation was suddenly revealing. In childhood she heard of a man in the village who would return from work and 'take' his wife on the hearth rug by the open fire. Hannah considered it rather coarse but found it equally exciting.

Most memorable, was when her father had to sack Charlie the cowman. It was noticeable one of their female calves had become "well developed at the back!" meaning the young creature's vulva was becoming too luscious for its age. The young cow had been 'experiencing' premature activity from the cowman who had found somewhere to shoot his semen! The animal's sensuous vulva would have rivalled anything offered by a woman.

As a teenager, Hannah's witnessing of mating animals led to her abiding judgement that all men were stallions! She recalled a visiting male being brought to her father's breeding mare in the 1920's. The two beasts met in the farmyard for the first time, exchanging a few sniffs and snorts while their respective owners held on to the reins. Her father's prize mare soon spread her back legs, excitedly, while a farmhand held her tail aside, revealing a sudden, slippery passage to entice the stallion.

"He was hung the size of my forearm" she said "and on he climbed and up it went out of sight and he did the job in no time at all. Father's mare just whinnied and out he came, dripping semen everywhere but there was a lovely foal after eleven months!"

Discussing sexual matters was no longer taboo. She always knew when I found "the right spot" but had never known it as her clitoris. Full intrusion of her vagina would be avoided while it needed dilation.

There was no suggestion that my 'willy' was too big for her, assuming there was ample capacity and she would take me eventually. She understood that a woman's genitalia was sometimes called a quim. The word of doubtful origin was around in the eighteenth century although later, in Victorian times, it generally referred to the fluid issuing from the vagina. She was just glad there was somewhere for me to "shoot my seed" and dreamed of feeling semen shooting into her.

Hannah's quickened breathing rendered further conversation impossible. She lost her grip on my cock and just had energy enough to pull me over on to her as she spread her legs without a word being uttered. My semen was dripping enough to anoint her vulva with the most natural lubrication to allow insertion of all my fingers while my thumb found her protruding clitoris.

I gambled luck by whispering a reminder of her obsession that all men were like stallions. Far from her being offended I had found a psychological spot. An increase in her breathless murmuring and the spontaneous contractions in her vagina that followed confirmed the fantasy she had harboured all those years and brought her to orgasm.

In jest, I whispered she might need a stallion to fully satisfy her now instead of fingers! Surprisingly, she shuddered and chuckled at my suggestion of this improbable act but I had unlocked the way to her desires.

I had stumbled on Hannah's fantasy and she was a little embarrassed. For the sake of the disgusted and uninitiated, Hannah would never have performed her fantasy, otherwise it would cease to be a fantasy! But such feelings had been around since Adam and Eve if we recourse to the Holy Bible. Leviticus, of Old Testament fame, issued harsh warnings for men or women who might think of 'lying down' with an animal.

Whenever I felt need to rouse her in the early hours she responded to my intrusion as though I had never been away. The invitation was endorsed the moment she felt my breath on her face. After a few moments of embracing we would assume the agreeable position of laying on our left sides. I could reach over her torso and slide my hand over the cushion-like Mons Pubis and part the outer labia of her moist vulva.

Episodes of playful dilation had enabled full penetration. But comfortable face to face intercourse with Hannah had proved awkward due to her bulging belly, making 'Venus Observa' less desirable. We contentedly contorted ourselves to caress, in this 'spooning' position, with Hannah striving over her right shoulder while I raised myself so our lips could meet.

Gentle stimulation of her clitoris soon caused her to lose coherence. She would indicate a gentle orgasm; with quickening breaths becoming exhaustively heavier until I felt her vaginal contractions urge my probing fingers. At this point, upon her barely coherent prompting, I would reposition to grasp her hips and lean back to thrust as she consumed and sapped the entire outcome of my penetration.

Daytime sessions became more rampant when I was at home on my shift-work pattern. We would take baths, to relax and make ourselves fully ready. We bathed and showered together whenever possible but the anticipation and excitement meant we often never made it to the bedroom! The answer was to introduce Hannah to a 'dildo' to prolong the session. She would be unable to draw premature ejaculations from a toy!

Hannah had never seen a prosthetic penis. I was risking fate as not all woman are willing to accept such things. I considered myself well versed in all fun crazes for experimental lovers through my time in Soho, the heart of the film and sex industry. Alison and I had experienced such playfulness for many years and now her mother would benefit.

At the sight of this 'new toy' Hannah was highly amused with an apt reaction: "There can't be much life in that thing!" admitting she had no idea that such things existed. I suggested she grasped it for a while, with her eyes closed, and she agreed it was realistic.

As I coaxed her to lay back, naked, with legs splayed over the edge of the bed all she had to do was trust me. My notion was to make a gentle, gradual and patient incursion for however long it might take. She considered it slightly bigger than my own erection, which was intentional, so this penetration had to be safe and gentle.

I anointed the dildo with a sensual lubricant and carefully presented it, burrowing between the lips of her vulva. Without forcing, she gradually consumed the toy up to its testicular hilt and I began gentle, rhythmic movements of penetration, which soon turned her panting to gasps. Her only concern was that I might lose it inside her, as she uttered that I was making her feel "as big as a pit-hole"!

"Pit hole" belonged to sexual vernacular of the past. Colloquially, it was a muddy pit, found mostly on farms to take surface and drainage water to prevent flooding. But today she was describing the sensation in her suddenly capacious vaginal canal. She was at last spreading to take her stallion!

I maintained the prosthetic's gentle inward thrusting and retracting. Its silicone makeup was faithful to the feel of the real thing. At each draw back her vagina's contractions were holding on, quite naturally and not letting go. It was more proof that she had nothing wrong 'down there'.

Breathless, and even less coherent than usual, she ordered me to "Get that thing out and put yourself in!" I calmed her to be patient by enlightening her of the variants in names given to vaginas in "The Perfumed Garden" telling her she was endowed with El taleb (the yearning one):

"This vagina is met within a few women only. With some it is natural; with others it becomes what it is with long abstinence. It is burning for a member, and, having got one in its embrace it refuses to part with it until its fire is completely extinguished"

She was certainly blessed with a yearning one and my technique had worked. I gently withdrew the false phallus, as her vaginal passage had strengthened its hold then immediately reposition myself to take its place in continuity. Entering Hannah on this occasion was the best ever, augmented by her vaginal convulsions. She orgasmed just ahead of my semen arriving as destined. The excitement for me was not in the deed but simply the thrill of bringing a seventy six year old to a state she had yearned for.

Hannah confided she had always dreamed of this day and was enjoying the activity now more than any other time in her life. She constantly reminded me of the day in 1963 when I ran up the road to ask the way to the farm. I had set her pulse racing but I was now nervous that I had ignited a fire which could burn beyond my control.

This liaison with Hannah was more than just a place to shoot my semen. I had bonded with the past; her memory of two world wars;

every experience of normal life in marriage and the scars of giving birth which could have rendered this relationship impossible.

In due course I performed a juggling act as I flittered between mother and daughter. Hygiene became the ultimate consideration so scrupulous bathing became ritualistic

Our couplings exploded many myths of age divisions. I had proved a woman's desire can remain deep below the surface, regardless of age, until the elements of rekindling are aligned. Her only anxiety was knowing I was satisfactorily "seeing after" Alison at the same time. It was an admirable and honourable concern.

Into the fourth year a monthly liaison with Hannah kept her at ease. The shift pattern of my work proved convenient, with some months seeing me at home every other day, alternating with fourteen hour days. The alternate days off provided generous opportunity and excuse for bedroom retreats, even when I needed some rest!

Appreciating each other's nakedness became commonplace. Women had long admired their own nude body but very few were aware of the attractiveness they revealed when stooping and seen from the rear. Like this, the vulva presented a new stance, more inviting, revealing its vertical lips much longer than when viewed frontally. Hannah, in this position, could bring out the stallion in any man if positioning herself animal-like on all fours.

In time, Hannah's desires became widely spaced and occasionally desperate. I could detect when a need was manifesting by her mood change and the onset of depression which she would make known to me. Gentle conversation and petting soon revealed what was on her mind leading to arousal and retreat to a convenient place; a sofa, a dining chair or even the stairs, if there was no time to make it to the bedroom! In married life she had to accept her husband's impulsive needs but now she was leading, encouraging and participating, making up for a lifetime of missed opportunities.

There was an occasion when I had risen early to clear the remnants of the previous evening's dinner when guests had been entertained. I was in a bath robe and Hannah came down in her dressing gown to help. I made tea and we sat at the table to comment and recall pleasantries of the previous evening meal before preparing breakfast. It had been some weeks since our last encounter and I surmised she was anxious. I was familiar with the signals.

We trusted the rest of the house was in deep slumber. I repositioned my chair a little further from the table and invited her to sit face to face, astride my lap, having opened my bath robe. Her legs were placed wider apart than usual and she took hold of my erection to guide entry with ease, her anticipation having produced natural secretions. Hannah's sudden vaginal contractions drew everything from me and our simultaneous orgasms left us breathless. This was another first but the scribe of "The Perfumed Garden" had warned of its dire consequences:

"If you do it with the woman bestriding you, your dorsal cord will suffer and your heart will be affected; and if in that position the smallest drop of the usual secretions of the vagina enters your urethral canal, a painful stricture may supervene"

But I trusted the countering comments of another translator who deciphered the quotation as nonsense due to superstitions of the time. And far from any injurious concern I was managing to keep two women happy.

Chapter 13

Hannah was now in her eighties and to the world at large my extra marital liaison with her was discreet. I took her on visits to her sister's house and encouraged her to welcome visitors in return. She was occasionally concerned about anyone knowing what we were doing so I constantly assured her that it was not their business; we were not breaking any laws and providing she was happy they could go away and multiply without my help! We were making the rules!

But one day I had cause for concern. Alison's circle of acquaintances included a lady who purported to be a medium and she raised concerns for Hannah's breathing! It was some time since our friend had visited and Hannah's 'breathing patterns', as 'heavy' as they could be on occasions, were well within her control and unlikely to have been heard in the next village, two miles away! Her orgasms were always measured and quiet, without extolling virtues of the Almighty! So what did our friend think she knew?

On mentioning the concern to Hannah she retorted with her favourite adage: "They can't catch an old bird with chaff!" Our 'medium' was aware I was at home every other day and Hannah always seemed to be happy and contented, alone with me! We both knew what was being suggested by our friend's concern but I felt it honourable to have consideration for anything untoward I might be causing Hannah.

Mediums were normally unwelcome in my life; less welcome than Jehovah's Witnesses. Mankind's final hang-up is generally fear of the unknown so therein lies the opening for budding clairvoyants. Hannah dismissed their skills as more 'bum-holes', so to call the bluff of our friendly clairvoyant, we agreed on a plan. I arranged a thorough health check as she had faith in our devoted family doctor and he appreciated my concerns.

Apart from Hannah's encroaching arthritis our practitioner complimented her fine health. Her lung condition and breathing were exceptional but he made one surprisingly, welcome suggestion while examining troublesome veins in her legs; swap the restrictive hosiery and girdle for something healthier! Surprisingly I was able to thank our friendly medium for her concern without telling her what a favour she had done for us.

Taking our doctor's advice, substituting the undergarments, was liberating. Hannah had long abandoned suspenders as 'mucky things', in favour of fashionable tights, ushered in by the arrival of the mini skirt. She still needed a supporting girdle, only this time, a more fashionable version, with suspenders to attach support stockings, just as she had worn twenty years earlier. I risked being branded selfish in being afforded easier access but the benefit for her soon became obvious during daylight hours! Widowhood had robbed her of almost everything but sensuous desire.

After a few months more it was time to summarise our gratifying liaison. Alison accepted her mother was under good control while my ever present concern was that Hannah was not taking me through duty. She often made comments about being happy to give me relief. She assumed her body did not provide the same comfort as that of her daughter but hoped I was enjoying 'the change of scenery'. Originally, I had set out to sup on her years of experience but more often I was teaching her new tricks and she enjoyed the arrangement.

She became thrilled that I loved her nakedness; amazed that a young man could love an old woman. But she never worried about looks, always reminding me of her late husband's adage "You don't look at the mantle shelf when you're stoking the fire grate"! And she was totally aware of her vulva being like a freshly prised oyster; when the whole world would slurp on them without daring to mention what the real attraction was. Her late husband loved oysters and she hated them.

The subject of a sensuous oyster brought about Hannah's initiation of oral stimulation. The act of cunnilinctus was foreign to her until I introduced her to nothing less innocent than a wine coaster depicting a famous artist's rendition of the procedure between a man and a woman.

The ceramic coaster was a birthday present to Alison from work colleagues. It proffered the sexual positon best for Libran women! To associate one particular love-making posture to any of the Zodiac signs is rather conjecturable but Alison and her mother shared the sign of Libra with birthdays just one week apart. It was a playful suggestion.

The picture was based on a drawing by Hungarian artist Mihaly Zichy (1827-1906). Milhaly's erotic renditions became famous after his death, two years before Hannah was born. Upon examining this particular 'making love, face sitting', Hannah's breath was taken away!

It portrayed a clothed man, supine, with a pretty girl straddling his torso with her long dress gathered into her arms well clear of her thighs to allow the partner to feast upon her vulva. It was pure erotica, typical Mihaly Zichy's work. During the nineteenth century he sketched couples in perfect sexual harmony along with classic female nudes, portraying more erotic atmosphere than many of today's photographs.

The act has never been regarded as unnatural having its original forms in most animals and common place amongst the earliest of races. Both sexes have long regarded the deed as the quintessential form of sexual pleasure, all part of the fondling process to induce arousal. The only time that cunnilinctus has been linked to perversion is when the act is preferred to full intercourse. But then if both partners are happy, why not?

Analysing the coaster's artwork had caused Hannah to tremble. She found it surprisingly wonderful that a man could do this to a woman but how could he tolerate doing it? Her only real concern was that she had 'come on' so quickly while my biggest thrill was knowing I had caused the state without touching her. We adjourned to the bedroom..

Hannah was not agile enough to straddle my supine torso. I gently laid her down onto the bed, above the coverings, with her legs splayed over the side. She was accustomed to my caressing and slipping down to draw upon her nipples. They protruded increasingly over the years but this day I went further, moving slowly from her breasts and let my tongue slither over her belly until I reached her vulva to caress the clitoris. Her steady breathing gradually increased to panting as she repeated what she had said earlier but this time, incoherently; "How you can stand doing that?" It was proof that Hannah had never experienced cunnilinctus and she had no intention of wanting me to stop.

Her orgasm was so powerful yet quiet and seemed interminable until she became exhausted and asked me to enter her. The oral stimulation had brought about a whole new state for her, as though her fulfilment might have gone on for ever. My accompanying excitement had caused a constant trickle of sperm yet my erection remained just strong enough to pass beyond her drenched labia and reach my own climax, instantly. Having experienced the benefit, Hannah accepted it was quite natural for the male to prepare a slippery passage. I never expected her to reciprocate the act; fellatio for the uninitiated

Hannah was always engrossed by my researching of sexual subjects. As a young woman she had wanted to be a schoolteacher and like myself, tended to treat any book on devoted subjects as a Bible. No longer was she taking everything lying down and was often stimulated simply by my conversation, without a single unruly member in sight!

Hanna delighted in recalling much of her marital past. She had resisted all attempts at pre-marital sex with her committed lover who tried to persuade her into retreating to the local secret hiding places. Even her father-in-law fancied his chances on one occasion and her brother-in-law felt all women's problems could be cured with 'a good poke'! All of them got nowhere until I came along and took the proper approach.

Months blossomed into years as we passed the milestones of birthdays. The periods between our passionate liaisons became longer, sometimes two months or more, until we arrived at Hannah's ninety second birthday. On this very morning she asked me to stay after taking breakfast to her in bed and wishing her the best of everything on her birthday.

By the time breakfast was over we were alone in the house. We began our well-practiced routine, culminating in a totally exhausting fulfilment for Hannah. But I sensed something was different as she turned to me and said quietly, "I think we should let well done alone". It had been almost sixteen years to the day since the first occasion and this was the last.

Over the years, Hannah had often mentioned presentiments. This very old and little used expression meant vague thoughts of foreboding situations; something she had witnessed with her acquaintances. She had experienced her own personal presentiment and slowly, but noticeably, she became weaker and spent long periods resting. In due course, she needed fulltime nursing so I gave her the care she was due and did so until she slipped gently away in February 2001.

Chapter 14

In these twilight years I find myself reflecting on the past. As the big parade of my life winds down I am witnessing accusations of misogyny, gender neutrality, sexual harassment and human misbehaviours; unfamiliar to me. As I gather the debris of my life's pageant and compare its gains and losses my one abiding issue is the policing and sanitizing of the English language.

Recently, I accidently broke a large jar of honey in the supermarket. After politely apologising to the young woman on the checkout, a male voice soon bellowed over the public address system, summoning "The Hygiene Team" to attend the exact spot where I was asked to remain standing. A queue formed of intrigued shoppers and stared inquisitively, waiting for some sort of mess to be wiped away, assuming I had thrown up or shit myself! Due to clumsiness of age I may have been shattered but not embarrassed! There was broken glass and honey galore. It just needed a bucket and mop! But then it would still require an 'operative', or in precise language, a cleaner!

On the other hand I am eternally grateful to life's hygienists for their clean-up of dirty weekends! Lovers' liaisons are now fully catered for in every sensual sense. Entire shelves in the pharmacy section of the same supermarket are now abundant with a countless variety of contraceptives; 'something for every weekend'. Everything is within the reach, even for the shortest lover and there are personal lubricants to assist comfortable entries, in forceful situations. Some playful products are so valuable they carry security devices, to prevent pilfering, like battery powered vibrators and clitoral stimulators. Fortunately, for me, they are not made of glass!

The supermarket can be a voyeur's paradise. 'The Perfumed Garden' pre-empted guidance for sexual union between people of all shapes and sizes who now promenade in great numbers along the aisles of the shopping mall. And I find it much healthier for the imagination. No more short skirts, daring to reveal packed vulvas but tight fitting denims, pulled over ample thighs, stretching tightly into ravine-like crotches. There maybe a few concerns for obesity but the women look very happy, generally accompanied by slim partners, a perfect match, with healthy toddlers in tow, just to prove that all has worked well. My ancestors believed they were nearer to God in a garden than anywhere else on earth, whereas I can enjoy my perfumed garden, sheltered from the elements.

Meanwhile, back to my future in 1949, I started school. Children of my generation knew nothing about saving the planet, protecting polar bears or adopting a snow leopard. As for old and flogged horses or distressed donkeys; they were taken to the knacker's yard to be minced into dog food. Global warming was unknown and climate change was something affecting a few rich people whenever they took foreign holidays.

Television was an infant with its solitary channel. The weak signals received in Norfolk came from the Midlands and I knew no one who owned a television receiver. This meant no endless scaremongering about anything. As for current headlines, telling us that we all bear some responsibility for clifftop houses falling into the sea, people of my generation regard it as the ultimate balderdash. And with the endless blame culture, comes the incomprehensible latest: cattle farting and belching! It's partly their fault, apparently!

Coastal erosion and its accompanying catastrophes have been part of local history for centuries. At primary school, we learned how the earth was getting warmer, the poles were still melting and the sea level would be much higher by the time our class reached old age. It did concern us as parts of our region's inland coastline lay very few feet above normal tide levels.

In 1954 I was ten and my teacher prepared me for the future I am experiencing. I was taught how the world was still evolving from the effects of the Ice Age and it all seemed quite feasible. The eroding Norfolk coastline had taken more than one church and village into the sea along with the entire town of Shipden in the 14th century. In 2023 the coastline is still eroding, having taken nearly all belief in God with it. During my childhood, old folk believed they could hear the undersea bells of lost churches ringing out warnings before a storm.

Further down the Suffolk coast the entire ancient city of Dunwich had disappeared. In Anglo Saxon times it was the capital of the Kingdom of the East Angles and at its peak boasted a port equal to 14th century London.

Our grandparents and parents had been taught prophesies of one Mother Shipton. She was a medieval mystic who predicted there would be little difference between summer and winter, eventually, while mankind would become weaker and wiser.

Mother Shipton's birthplace at Knaresborough in Yorkshire is a tourist attraction these days. She forecast situations and inventions which current scholars interpret as having reached fruition. Her prophesy that words would flash round the world like lightning is now seen as her forecasting modern telephony, or even the WorldWideWeb, although modern analysts still scrutinise surviving manuscripts to judge authenticity. But some documents, allegedly compiled after her death, along with her prophesy of the end of the world in 1881, put her soothsaying into doubt.

Saving the planet from global warming is the new Mammon. But who will be left to inherit the earth as I learn now the world sperm count is falling! It will be an almighty task but not for my generation, raised in the era when people feared God. We were ensured of a good life if we trusted in him and kept our bowels open!

Whenever my lifestyle is questioned I quote the perennial line from "The Go-Between", J P Hartley's famed novel, "The past is a foreign country; they do things differently there". They do, or perhaps we did, but everyone is enjoying unashamed fun these days!

About the Author

J ames Ayton was born during the latter stages of World War II, at Newmarket, Suffolk, where his father was a Royal Air Force conscripted medic. James' working life with post production in broadcast television gave him a lifestyle never envisaged by his pious ancestors. He inherited his name from great-uncle, James Ayton, a pioneering immigrant to Seattle, Washington at the turn of the 19th century.

www.ingramcontent.com/pod-product-compliance
Lightning Source LLC
Chambersburg PA
CBHW021021160726
47994CB00006B/2610